WOMEN OF FAITH IN DIALOGUE

Women of Faith
in Dialogue

edited by

Virginia Ramey Mollenkott

CROSSROAD • NEW YORK

1988

The Crossroad Publishing Company
370 Lexington Avenue, New York, N.Y. 10017

Printed in the United States of America

Library of Congress Cataloging in Publication Data

Women of faith in dialogue.

1. Women and religion. I. Mollenkott, Virginia R.
BL458.W585   1987   291'.088042   87-8843
ISBN 0-8245-0823-8

Acknowledgments

"Gather Us In," words and music by Marty Haugen, © 1982
by G.I.A. Publications, Inc. Reprinted by permission.

For Inge Lederer Gibel,
who first brought us together
and still provides
inspiration.

"And what can we do, a few women whom the world listens to less than it should? Continue talking to each other, and others; continue hearing and caring about each other's stories, as we have in the past; keep widening the circle, keep building bridges, overcoming barriers, turning the other into the human. This method, I painfully acknowledge, is not as quick, currently fashionable, or immediately effective as bombs and guns. But I still believe. I still believe."

— Inge Lederer Gibel,
in a letter from Jerusalem,
5 September 1986

Contents

EDITOR'S PREFACE: VIRGINIA RAMEY MOLLENKOTT   1

WOMEN OF FAITH AND THIS VOLUME:
JEANNE AUDREY POWERS   3

**Part One: A Dialogue concerning the Diversity
of Who We Are and the Tasks We Face**   7

1   A Meeting of the Minds
    Sarah Cunningham   9

2   Confrontation and Change:
    Women and the Jewish Tradition
    Blu Greenberg   17

3   Change and Confrontation
    within the Roman Catholic
    Church
    Ann Patrick Ware   29

4   A Polish-American Catholic
    Perspective
    Delphine Palkowski   42

5   An Asian-American Woman
    Reflects on Racism, Classism,
    and Sexism
    Naomi P. F. Southard   51

6   An Evangelical Perspective on
Interreligious Dialogue
Virginia Ramey Mollenkott   61

**Part Two: A Dialogue concerning Our Struggles
within Our Own Religious Communities**   75

7   The Call of Women in the
Church Today
Rosemary Radford Ruether   77

8   The Struggle of a Black Lutheran
Mary L. Chrichlow   89

9   Women in the Context of Change
and Confrontation within Muslim
Communities
Riffat Hassan   96

10   Racism, Classism, and Sexism: A
Jewish Woman's Perspective
Ellen M. Umansky   110

**Part Three: A Dialogue on Working Together
for Justice in the World**   121

11   Working Together
Eva Catafygiotu Topping   123

12   A Rationale for Coalition
Building
Ann Gillen   127

13   Judaism, Feminism, and Peace in
the Nuclear Age
Sheila Peltz Weinberg   143

14   Anti-Semitism and Its Role in
     International Politics
       Inge Lederer Gibel   152
15   A Black Woman's Perspective on
     Racism, Classism, Sexism, and
     Ageism
       Elizabeth M. Scott   165
16   The Feminization of Poverty
       Mimi Alperin   170

Part Four: An Interreligious Worship Service   **177**

17   Preparing an Interreligious
     Worship Service
       Norma U. Levitt   179
18   Gathering: An Interreligious
     Worship Service   184

*Appendix: Guidelines for Forming a
Local Group of Women of Faith*   193

Preface

This book represents dialogue among women from various branches of the three monotheistic religious traditions: Judaism, Christianity, and Islam. Specifically, this book represents three different dialogues: on the diversity of who we are and the tasks we face; on the struggles women face *within* our own faith-communities; and on working together to achieve justice in the world at large.

Readers who are looking for a collection of conversations in which various women exchange brief remarks will be disappointed. There may be a need for such a book, but I find that sort of interaction easier to participate in than to read. Instead, this book presents dialogue in the sense of an exchange of sustained ideas or opinions about a topic. The result looks like a collection of essays, and it is — but with this difference: that every author speaks consciously and personally out of her own faith-experience, making that experience central to her perception of the topic at hand.

Although many women have left the biblical religions out of disgust at the inequities within those traditions, we who have contributed to this book have not (perhaps in some cases, not *yet*) felt it our calling to make that departure. We respect the integrity of our sisters who are involved in alternative forms of feminist spirituality; but for the most part we have chosen to stay within our religious traditions and to work for justice from the inside.

This book was made possible in part by a grant from the Milton and Selma Feld Foundation of Kansas City, Missouri. Initial editing was done by a committee consisting of Sister

Joan Ronayne, Sarah Cunningham, Mimi Alperin, and Virginia Baron. My thanks to them for providing a foundation upon which I could build.

Virginia Ramey Mollenkott

Women of Faith
and This Volume
∾
Jeanne Audrey Powers

Judy Chicago, referring to her ceramic-and-tapestry tribute to women, *The Dinner Party*, has written:

> The women represented are either historical or mythological figures. I have brought them together—invited them to dinner, so to speak—that we might hear what they have to say and see the range and beauty of a heritage we have not yet had an opportunity to know. All institutions of our culture tell us—through words, deeds, and even worse, silence—that we are insignificant. But our heritage is our power.

It is precisely this heritage that brought together women from Protestant, Catholic, Jewish, and Muslim communities of faith to participate in a conference called Women of Faith in the 80s. This heritage brings us together now to produce this book. We believe that women in our religious traditions have seldom been "invited to dinner" together, and that

---

The Reverend Dr. Jeanne Audrey Powers is the associate general secretary of the United Methodist Church's General Commission on Christian Unity and Interreligious Concerns. She has served on numerous committees of the World Council of Churches, the National Council of Churches, and the Consultation on Church Union. Ordained in 1957 just one year after women's ordination was approved by the United Methodist Church, Dr. Powers has championed the role of clergywomen in decision making in her denomination.

there is much we do not know about one another. Therefore, this book is an invitation to you, the reader, to sit at that same table, and to discover your power in our common, yet multifaceted, heritage.

Our struggle to discover this power has not always been easy. The Decade for Women Conference in Mexico City in 1975 was a very painful one for many Jewish women when international political issues challenged their deeply held religious convictions and identity. At the U.S. Conference on Women held in Houston in 1977, American women reacted to the difficulties in Mexico by forming a coalition to support one another on issues that concerned religion. Particularly, they wanted to affirm their commitment to an atmosphere of respect and openness toward all women, honoring each person's heritage, tradition, and ethnic and cultural origins; and they wanted to resist all efforts to pit one culture or religious tradition against another for purely political reasons.

Late in the 1970s, as a representative group from the New York area, women of faith from the Jewish, Christian, and Islamic religious traditions began to meet on a regular basis. They sought a better understanding of each other's commitments, and an engagement in dialogue on some of the issues related to their religious perspectives. Sometimes their meetings resulted in cooperative action. Nearly always they included the sharing of resources — personal and material — among women in the group.

As a result of the growing trust among them they began to make plans for a "Women of Faith in the 80s" conference to enable more women from throughout the country to share in the experience of women's interreligious dialogue. The first conference was held at Stony Point, New York, in November 1980; a second was held at Marymount College in Virginia in January 1984. This volume includes some of the major papers from these conferences.

Some of the authors included here — Ann Patrick Ware, of the Sisters of Loretto; Inge Lederer Gibel, of the American Jewish Committee; and Sarah Cunningham, then of the Presbyterian women's magazine *Concern* — participated in a women's interreligious dialogue on the Middle East in 1974. The dialogue served as a catalyst for a 1976 seminar in the Middle East that included women from both Jewish and Christian traditions. These efforts led to the founding of the Women of Faith Task Force.

Protestant laywomen and clergywomen, Catholic women religious and religious women, and women rabbis and lay women from four streams of Jewish traditional religious life have all been active on the task force. With the addition of Dr. Riffat Hassan of the University of Louisville, a Muslim scholar specializing in the rediscovery of the heritage of women in the Quran, the three monotheistic religious traditions were represented. The two Women of Faith conferences, assisted by a major grant from the Nathan Appleman Institute for the Advancement of Christian-Jewish Understanding, have utilized members of the task force in leadership roles. These women represent a variety of professions: editors, scholars, administrators, professors, journalists, authors. Some are more closely associated with institutions than others, but each stands firmly in her own religious tradition, with concern to criticize its perspectives on women and to offer its wisdom as a gift to others.

Interreligious dialogue is never easy. When participants around the table hold conflicting convictions, the task is infinitely more difficult: perspectives on Israel, on inclusive language, on abortion, on homosexuality, on Soviet Jewry, and on concepts of feminism have each been sources of conflict even among members of a single religious tradition. But because each participant knows what it means for women to be silenced or rendered insignificant in her own tradition, a special kind of hearing and openness in listening takes place.

Sensitivity toward differing positions is crucial in dialogue, and the common experiences of women that run through all of the traditions make dialogue uniquely possible for women.

It is in that spirit that this book has been published. As dialogue, the essays here are an invitation to dialogue. They come out of the deep experiences of women in their various religious traditions. And they are offered in the strong conviction that in our heritage is our power.

PART ONE

A Dialogue concerning the Diversity of Who We Are and the Tasks We Face

Presbyterian Sarah Cunningham leads off this discussion with a description of the tasks, demands, commonalities, and challenges of interreligious dialogue. She is followed by Blu Greenberg, who presents the glories and the inequities of being a woman in Orthodox Judaism, and confesses a yearning for those "surges of the spirit" that are difficult to experience in the midst of the struggle for justice.

Sister Ann Patrick Ware describes the anguished disappointment of many Catholics with John Paul II's resolute denial of justice to women, and she discusses the transformation of the Sisters of Loretto from a hierarchical structure to one that is collegial and egalitarian, indeed a model for the larger society. From the perspective of a Roman Catholic laywoman, Delphine Palkowski describes the life of a third-generation Polish-American and calls for an assimilation process that respects rather than diminishes ethnic identity.

The Reverend Naomi P. F. Southard, a United Methodist clergywoman, describes the injustices endured by Asian-Americans and by women within the Asian-American subculture, calling for a transformation that she is certain will eventually take place.

Finally, Virginia Mollenkott, a Protestant evangelical, describes the evangelical political spectrum, suggests ways of transcending the evangelical drive to proselytize, and outlines her understanding of the tasks facing contemporary women of faith.

1

A Meeting of the Minds

Sarah Cunningham

We gather at this conference as Women of Faith, women of Jewish, Christian, and Muslim traditions who are heirs to a history that connects us all to common ancestors in the faith. We belong to the long line of those who have dreamed dreams and told tales of a God who creates and nourishes us, who asks us who we are, and what we are doing, and where we are going. We belong to the people who claim to "go out" at God's bidding, who make journeys, who build cities, who seek futures blessed by God. We are admonished to love our neighbors and to seek peace, and we prophesy that someday we will dwell together in harmony, love, justice, and good-will.

In that spirit we bring to our conscious awareness both that which unites us and that which separates us. We agree to live with this awareness for a time while we also talk of

SARAH CUNNINGHAM has served as associate editor of *A.D.* magazine, a national publication for the United Presbyterian Church and the United Church of Christ. She has also edited *Concern*, a quarterly journal and monthly bulletin for United Presbyterian women, and several other publications. She currently serves as a deacon at Riverside Church. She has written articles for Protestant, Catholic, and Jewish publications, and is a lecturer and consultant on church-related issues.

our common task, which we address not only by asking who we are but also, "What will we do together?" and "What are our expectations for the future?"

All of us are just the right women for such a meeting of minds as this conference. But while we make this assertion, we are aware that there are countless other women who would also be "just right" for this task.

We are not an officially representative body. We came together in a much less formal and less structured way. Even though we do belong to major religious organizations within the United States, we are by no means either an official gathering or a totally representative one for these organizations. We are one expression of that very important configuration, the ad hoc coalition. We are a group of women who have come together at this time out of common interests and common concerns. We have crossed boundaries, sought new alliances, broken new ground. As we discover that what we are about is good and has potential for the future, we will find ways to share it and to establish networks for its continuation.

While I was thinking about this meeting of minds, it occurred to me as a Protestant — and I think Catholics would also agree — that we Christians are so numerous in this country and so prolific in generating projects within our own constituencies that we sometimes forget to ask how we are doing in matters of interreligious dialogue or certain community projects that demand interreligious participation if they are to succeed. On the whole, we Christian women spend most of our energies carrying out our own regional, national, and international agendas. On the secular level, we note such large-scale endeavors as the International Decade for Women and the International Women's Year, and we endorse the large celebrations and movements of women, but we fail to ask frequently enough what we as women of faith could do across religious lines.

Women of America's smaller religious constituencies, whether Jewish, Muslim, or some other—including, perhaps, the third-world women's caucuses in all our faiths—know how important it is to keep the dialogue going, to build the coalitions, to work together across religious and ethnic boundaries. They initiate such encounters even while, to some extent, fearing "co-optation" or the more threatening religious inclination toward proselyting (Christians in particular must ask serious questions these days about what their faith demands of them in relation to other religions. Are we called to seek conversion, or are we called to love, accept, serve, be open to, and learn from those of other religions—and to seek the common goals of a new creation?)

At any rate, we must all continually be grateful to those groups who are both small enough in size and universal enough in vision to know how important interreligious dialogue is for this world and for these times. It is a very lonely existence and a very isolated one, yes, even a threatening one, to be a member of a minority group and yet not be able to have honest, open, candid, and trusting dialogue with those of the dominant group.

This brings us, then, to the risks we take in a meeting of minds such as this. All of us come out of religious traditions that we love, honor, and care about deeply. Our religious roots have nourished us, given us our bearings, focused our energies, and helped us find life's transcendent meanings. We do not want those traditions weakened by a kind of relativism or syncretism that does not speak to our interior worlds in particular ways.

Yet we know we live in new times that demand new duties. We know that each of our traditions has within it a strong leaning toward universal wholeness, the unity of all creation, the common recognition of the One God of all. We must take our cues from that knowing—and take them seriously. Thus, each of us is compelled to seek out "the other."

We want very much to know what we can be and do together.

So, how will this event help us in that quest? During the few days we are gathered here, we will share concerns and we will listen to scholars, teachers, and specialists in areas of common concern. We will debate issues and discuss how we can enrich one another. We will ask new questions, and possibly find new answers and new mutual agendas.

In addition, there will be times to celebrate the fact that we are people who tell tales, who discover who we are by reciting our stories.

To some degree, I should think, all of us gathered here understand ourselves as the products of our histories. We are who we are today because of where we have come from. However, we are women of histories that have been heavily influenced by a masculine reading of time and events. And because our experiences as women have been different from those of men, and because, as we have read our stories of faith and reflected upon them, we have come to certain conclusions that are quite different from those of past inter-pretations, we are willing to entertain such ideas as these:

- All revelation about God is to some degree limited — not wrong, perhaps, but limited. The male image alone is not adequate.
- Any understanding of community that is hierarchical rath-er than egalitarian seems to us as women to be only partial-ly adequate for our times and for the future.
- A world that is still preoccupied with "taking sides," with the "just war," with weapons of total destruction, with sending "sons" off to be killed while assuming it is the more humane thing to insist that women stay home and mourn and wait and rebuild after the destruction, cannot be the world of justice that is adequate for tomorrow.

In other words, women have insights and ask questions. When we come together, we find common bonds among ourselves as women of faith. In the commonality of what we have been denied in each of our separate traditions, we find a strange kind of unity. And in such an atmosphere, we dare to wonder aloud whether the forefathers were not somehow and sometimes fallible in the teachings they handed down to us regarding the totality of what God might be up to on this earth. Consequently, we dare to be open to "new things."

Now, having acknowledged the importance of telling tales as a means of finding out who we are and what we can do together, I will tell briefly one of my own — a tale of religious pilgrimage — as a means of reflecting on the events that have brought me to this place and to certain expectations for a meeting of minds such as this.

I recall an experience of twenty-odd years ago, when I was a student at Union Theological Seminary in New York City. I was struggling with what now seems a very simple question, but which was then the religious question of my life. It was the question of whether I had the freedom to move beyond the tradition into which I had been born to find a religious vocation in the larger world.

I grew up in the Bible Belt, in a small town in western Tennessee where the main Presbyterian church was affiliated with the Cumberland Presbyterian denomination, a small branch of Presbyterianism. My distant cousin was the pastor of my local church, and I felt very secure as a part of that congregation. The church was well regarded by the community and, as far as I was concerned, it was right for me. There was a small Presbyterian U.S. (Southern) church in town and an even smaller black Presbyterian church, but we were a very segregated community, both racially and religiously, and, like all those around me, I made an uneasy peace with that reality.

My particular denomination took root in the Cumberland plateau of Tennessee and Kentucky during the early nineteenth century. By the beginning of the twentieth century, the majority of its members decided it had accomplished its purpose as a separate denomination and voted to go back into the "mother" church (Presbyterian U.S.A.) from which it had "seceded." But there was a remnant that decided not to do that. It was into this branch that I was baptized as a child, and in which I later found my vocation as an editor of church-school materials.

When I eventually came to Union Theological Seminary, I was making quite a theological and ecclesiastical leap. I had already "left home" in a secular sense, but, having chosen a church-related vocation, to leave the church where that vocation was first begun felt like betrayal, and it made me very uneasy. Nevertheless, I was challenged, disturbed, and fascinated by overwhelming questions of faith and the search for ultimate and universal meanings. For a time that search diminished for me the significance of particularities.

There came an evening when certain questions of faith finally found their answers. I was attending a play produced by Union's drama department, a retelling of the Genesis story of Adam and Eve. I do not recall being terribly impressed with the play's interpretation of the story, but I do recall that the events of the evening triggered my imagination in such a way that I began to think about the story of the Garden of Eden in a totally new way.

This is the power of biblical literature: the stories have the power to mean different things to different people, depending on the questions one brings to them at the time. My question that evening was one I had been asking long before I came to the play, but I was still awaiting its answer. My question was: Did I have the right, and the freedom, and the courage, to leap into the unknown?

The answer came to me that evening through a new perspective on the Genesis story. It was inevitable that Eve and Adam would leave the Garden of Eden. They had to take the risk of going out, of eating of the tree of knowledge (of good

and evil), of whatever that tree of further exploration represented for them. They had to leave innocence behind and
move on, even at the risk of displeasing, deserting, and *defy-
ing* God.

This was what was happening in my own life. On the one
hand, I felt pressure within to go back home. There I was
loved, needed, and in a sense "possessed." Saying no to that
was difficult: it left at loose ends a lot of crazy pieces of my
particular puzzle. But after that particular confrontation
with the Genesis story, I understood my dilemma clearly and
chose my response. I had to leave my Garden of Eden, even
if by doing so I was saying no to God.

By taking that risk, what I really learned in time was that
when one dares to explore the larger reality, the world be
yond innocence and beyond one's own particular knowing at
any given time, the God of the universe does not turn away
or recede into the unknown. God did not leave me desolate.
Rather, at least for me, God was still there, alongside me,
even ahead of me. God was, is, and shall be.

That experience was my initiation into a faith that did not
have to have absolute answers anymore. It was a faith of
knowing, of trust, of presence, and a faith that said it is
truth that will set us free: not dogmas, or creeds, or boxes, or
even a secure place, but truth.

I must hasten to add that, for me, this journey toward the
truth (toward the "new") does not demand a rejection of
one's past, of one's particular story, of one's particular tradition. No, never that. It is very important to know who you
are, and where you have come from — to claim your story.
(This is one thing the Christian zealot is always slow to
learn: that is, how important roots are, and how devastating
it is to cause another to reject totally a past tradition for the
sake of being "born anew").

In my own case, I am still to some degree a Cumberland
Presbyterian. I am still to some degree a small-town South-

erner. It is from that base that all my knowing comes. But I am also a citizen of the world, a pilgrim of all time and eternity, and this, too, I must affirm. (I recall a conversation with a friend years ago in which she explained to me that it was when she was able to claim her ancestry of slavery that she also began to understand her journey into freedom. It is this understanding of one's roots that I speak of here).

So, we are gathered as an interreligious group, first of all to claim who we are. We have no desire to be converted, syncretized, or amalgamated into anything else. But we are also here to testify to the difference between knowing and claiming our story on the one hand, and being a slave to its limitations on the other. We refuse to restrict God to our own particulars.

All our stories prepare us for this new chapter in our lives, for leaping into the unknown dimensions of interreligious dialogue. Only as we move into such a dialogue can we find out what the future holds for such a venture. We can expect new questions, new knowings, new levels of trust in one another, new affirmations of faith.

Perhaps we will also find some very specific, pragmatic, and particular next steps toward each other, with each other, and beyond ourselves toward all others.

2

Confrontation and Change: Women and the Jewish Tradition

Blu Greenberg

When you have labored for what seems to be a long time for issues that concern women of faith, you may begin to experience an emotional and spiritual burnout. Sometimes, even if you strive quietly and gently, the spiritual ties that bind begin to fray. Sometimes, the energy used for vigilance begins to sap your own religious strength and integrity. Sometimes, you confront the traditional sources you love so much, and find them wanting. And resistant. Sometimes, experimentation in ritual that gives women greater expression seems to generate more self-consciousness than it does connection to the holy. These are restless times — and though I feel optimistic about the future, I feel restless too.

I must confess with some sadness that while I follow the mitzvot (the tenets of Judaism) with care, and while I feel a great and close affinity for my own community (that of

BLU GREENBERG, who has studied in the Department of Religion at Columbia University, has published *On Women and Judaism* and *How to Run a Traditional Jewish Household*. She has also published many articles in Jewish and ecumenical periodicals and journals. Married to a rabbi and mother of five children, she is also active in community affairs.

Orthodox Judaism) I have not felt a surge of the spirit in a great while. And I long for it. Not all the time, but every once in a while. I long to be the deeply devout person I once was, in my more innocent life where everything God said was sacred and everything that was sacred was said by God. I know it has something to do with eating the apple and knowing. Yet I also know I can never go back. I would never want to.

Living in that tension, then, is the lot of women who are unwilling to say of Judaism or Christianity, "It is hopelessly antifeminist and, therefore, it is finished," or "We are finished with it." Instead, we choose to live in the creative tension that comes not of wanting to leave but rather of wanting to enter our faith-communities more fully.

There are certain basic premises we keep in mind as we take up the tasks of change and confrontation. I believe these premises are common to women of all faith communities, though I speak of them here in the language of my own community.

First, we understand that history and sociology, not just tradition, are normative or at least can be used as interpretive keys. Yet we also wrestle with other truths: that Torah and tradition stand by themselves, independent, outside of history. Revelation intersects history, yet remains apart from it. We must learn to move intelligently within that dialectic.

Second, we understand on a practical level the need to balance change and continuity. This is as important for the individual psyche as it is for community cohesion. Any religion that is reduced to social relativism isn't going to offer very much in the way of sacredness, anchors, roots, or a sense of existential security that comes of knowing where we are located and what is expected of us.

Third, we have learned that it is easier to destroy than to build up, so we are careful about what we choose to destroy.

Fourth, we feel a love and a protectiveness of our own

faith-community and its value system, even as we judge, nudge, criticize, and move ever farther beyond the perimeters that are so closely drawn. In fact, it is precisely because we feel primarily the connection and commitment and not the distance or disinterest that we stay within the community and do so many things that go against our grain or that cause discomfort in others.

Fifth, we know that there are times in the history of a faith-community when obedience through lack of pride is the greater sin, and unrestful rebellion is the greater merit. We will not be intimidated by those who want to dismiss us.

All this being so, trade-offs are the name of the game in confrontation and change within our faith-communities. For example, the Orthodox community has often been criticized for its retention of one of the early morning blessings recited by a male: "Blessed be Thou O Lord Ruler of the Universe, who hast not made me a woman." In a parallel prayer, a woman says, "Blessed be Thou O Lord Ruler of the Universe, who hast created me according to Thy will." (This latter blessing was added into the liturgy more than a thousand years after the first prayer—a symbol of both problem and progress).

Although contemporary defenders of the male morning blessing offer apologetic exegesis (leaning heavily on the benign tradition that man is superior only insofar as he is obligated by more commandments), I am compelled to say that the blessing is sexist in tone if not in original intent—and my own belief is that it was indeed sexist in intent. I, too, can cite a few traditional commentaries in support of my interpretation. Yet I have a real dilemma here. For I must acknowledge that those Jews who point to sexism in the morning blessing are the same ones who long ago gave up saying that blessing, or any other of the morning blessings, which go as follows:

Blessed be Thou, Lord our God, King of the Universe, who hast given the rooster intelligence to distinguish between day and night.
   . . . who hast not made me a heathen
   . . . who hast not made me a slave
   . . . who hast not made me a woman [for men]
   . . . who hast made me according to Thy will [for women]
   . . . who opens the eyes of the blind
   . . . who clothes the naked
   . . . who sets the captives free
   . . . who raises up those who are bowed down
   . . . who spreads forth the earth above the waters
   . . . who has provided for all my needs
   . . . who guides the steps of man
   . . . who girds Israel with might
   . . . who crowns Israel with glory
   . . . who gives strength to the weary
   . . . who removes sleep from my eyes and slumber from my eyelids.

These blessings, as a whole, represent a kind of spiritual stretching exercise, where nothing is taken for granted. So while I hope to see the male blessing, authentic and ancient as it is, newly paraphrased in a way that doesn't suggest male hierarchy, I still continue to place my bets with the community that has not abandoned the daily liturgy or consigned it to a few of its rabbis. For all my quarrel with that blessing and what it symbolizes, I still prefer to identify with the community that understands and has taught me that one ought to give thanks to God for waking up alive, alert, and in good health, every single day of one's life. I know how hard it is to rebuild a habit of liturgy once it is destroyed. These are the trade-offs I must continually make.

There are two arenas for bringing about change. Both, of course, involve confrontation: one arena is tradition, and the other is community. Each is interdependent upon the other.

What does it mean to confront tradition, the sources, the sacred texts? How can one confront the Torah, Talmud, centuries of rabbinic interpretation, layers of haggadic and halachic material, centuries-old ethical and legal concepts, authoritative codes of law, and so forth? We confront, bringing to our study and our search the new theology of women, a new yardstick by which to understand our faith and history, and against which we test all the material therein. The new yardstick is the basic principle of feminism, that women are equal, created equally in the image of God, and therefore have equal potential, ability, and aspirations. This theology says that women must have a full equality in matters of mind, spirit, and deed.

I rather like this task of confronting tradition. It can be quite fruitful. It's amazing what rich veins there are to mine in an ancient tradition. In fact, confronting the sources provides much of the wherewithal for confronting community.

For me, this confrontation is a religious experience, a holy task in itself, one that binds me up with God and with the Jewish people, even though I come, so to speak, with a quarrel. In Judaism, study is equated with prayer. I have come to understand that that is no mere prescription. Rather, it is a very real description of human emotions involved in encountering sacred literature, no matter how critical the intellectual enterprise may be.

By means of the yardstick of women's equality we can trace how much reinterpretation the tradition has undergone in the course of two or three thousand years, particularly on women's issues. One example is Jewish divorce law. The Bible tells us that a man who wishes to divorce his wife must write a writ of divorce, put it in her hand, and send her away. We can understand this scriptural norm in two ways. We can view it simply as reflective of the sexism in the Bible, a male-oriented, patriarchal, patrilineal, patrilocal society, with men having all the initiative and making all the moves. But another way is to see it as the first step toward reducing male divorce rights and, hence, as a protection for women.

In the ancient Near East, a man, in a flash of anger or frustration, could pronounce orally his intent to divorce, and the woman was irrevocably divorced. Under those circumstances, a wife had to be very careful about challenging or confronting her husband; she had to take great care lest she displease him. Biblical law, however, required the formal drawing up of a writ of divorce. This operated as a delaying tactic, with the opportunity to frame each episode in the context of the total relationship—a strategy as necessary to the building of a marriage in these times as it was in those days. It was a small protection, but it signaled the direction Jewish divorce law was to take as it unfolded through history.

Rabbinic law includes all sorts of modifications of man's absolute rights: first, it required a man to show cause. He would not simply divorce a woman at will. (This however, was not necessarily always a protection for a woman, because once the cause of divorce was known, it would be less likely that she would find another husband). During rabbinic times, polygamy was de facto, and finally de jure, eliminated. In most cases, a woman could not be divorced against her will. The *ketubah* was formulated in rabbinic times: this was a marriage contract that stipulated all sorts of economic conditions to discourage divorce. The *ketubah* also protected a woman in marriage, specifying what her husband's obligations were to her. Dowry money was held in escrow for the wife. The rabbis could coerce a man, through the use of sanctions, into granting a divorce to a woman who wanted one. A court of law, in certain situations, was empowered to annul marriage. And so on.

Still, a great problem exists today in that a man still has the initiative and can withhold a divorce for selfish reasons.

But we know, as a consequence of applying our yardstick to the study of sources, that this is not at all what halacha wanted to achieve. We can say that Jewish law contains the well-tested principle of women's redress in cases of recalcitrant husbands. We can point to Jewish legal precedents and build upon them. For example, if talmudic law permits a woman to pay for the scribe to write the "man's" writ, the halachists of today must interpret the law to allow women to initiate, authorize, and deliver the Jewish divorce writ. There has been both logical and historical growth of women's rights in Judaism, and we must foster this by pointing out its roots in the religio-legal literature.

In some situations, confrontation can force a break or a reversal of the direction tradition has taken. For example, in the area of women and liturgy, or women and learning, tradition moves toward a limiting of women's formal expression. Women were at Sinai; they experienced the peak moment of revelation. But they were not invited back. As tradition unfolded, women historically were not found in the house of study, nor were they counted as members in good standing of the holy congregation. Only recently has this exclusion begun to change.

In these instances, we are obliged to summon forth the larger principles of equality of women and of women entering the tradition more fully. We have to articulate these in Jewish categories, and apply them creatively to ritual and religious expression. The basic premise is not that Revelation was wrong, for that would take us nowhere. Rather it is that God spoke to the community in terms appropriate to its understanding and its times; and for most of that history, the hierarchy of the sexes in matters of faith and authority was unchallenged. A theology of women, however, is not completely alien to the tradition. Nor is it new. It was and is God's ultimate plan. Moreover, there are many areas in the tradition where we see a movement from hierarchy to egalitarianism. As Jews, we affirm chosenness and the special election of the Jewish people, but we know this must include women as well as men.

In truth, there have been changes recently even in the areas that were historically associated with men only. Women can now find, here and there, communities that accommodate their spiritual needs by offering women's *minyanin* (prayer groups) and women's schools of higher learning. There has been an amazing explosion of women's encounter with sacred sources, exegesis, and halachic literature — encounters that were closed off to them for so long.

But what about confronting the community? That is the harder task, for, as we all know, even the best-intentioned religious establishment is slow to respond to change. Here, I would like to offer some personal guidelines, some thoughts about what works for me, or what would perhaps work better if I would stick to it.

First, our emphasis and energy should properly be directed toward real gains, not toward rhetoric (although you can't avoid rhetoric altogether). We cannot rewrite history, nor would we want to. Despite its limitations for women's issues, it is still sacred history. It is still the tradition that nurtured us, and that made us what we are as women of faith, and we cannot overlook that.

Therefore, don't denigrate it in the face of its believers. Don't overemphasize its negative parts. Don't waste precious time and energy debating the patriarchal nature of the religion. When we speak of women's place in Jewish tradition, we must tell the whole story, give a balanced picture, describe it in its totality. Jewish women were not deliberately oppressed or persecuted by Jewish men; in many instances they were highly regarded, honored, and protected. When we acknowledge this, our claims that women no longer want a pedestal or benign protectiveness and that inequity and discrimination still exist will be better understood. Without this understanding we might end up talking to ourselves.

Second, we must order our priorities. We cannot do everything, certainly not all at once. If we tried, it would certainly be very frustrating. I see five areas that need improvement, each one significant: learning, leadership, liturgy, legal status, and language. I have come to see that the most important area for Jewish women's religious equality is that of Jewish scholarship, culminating in the ordination of women. When that happens, I believe everything else will fall into place. My second most important area concerns women and Jewish divorce law. If one woman suffers as a result of the law, then the law discriminates against us all.

For the time being, I have simply neglected or temporarily abandoned the complex issue of language: for example the use of masculine pronouns in reference to God and to the holy community. Although I don't personally feel that God is male (despite the extensive use of male pronouns), the rewards of praying in the same words the exact prayer that Jews everywhere have used for two thousand years, means something very special to me. More would be lost than gained for me, I believe, at least in the transition stage, in changing from the familiar. Meanwhile, I read with great interest what others are doing in this area, and I acknowledge that a serious problem exists, but I don't attempt to enter into the controversy.

We have to learn from the women's movement to choose our political measures wisely. Those who say religion and politics should not be spoken in the same breath are not telling the whole story. The political process was often involved in the expansion of ritual.

There are all kinds of political methods we can use. Here is a story of passive resistance: A woman in Montreal wanted a divorce, and her husband would not grant her one. He

demanded twenty-five thousand dollars from her; she refused, and he withheld the divorce. Her friends were horrified at the situation, so thirty of them, all religious women in
the Orthodox community, banded together and announced
that none of them would go to the *mikveh* (the ritual bath)
until the woman was granted a writ of divorce. Those of you
who are familiar with Jewish law know that sexual relations
cannot be resumed after a woman's menses until she has gone
to the *mikveh*. Need I say more? That was the fastest divorce
ever granted in the history of Montreal's religious community!

Although the solution of one case for one woman does not
solve the whole problem, the idea of organizing and using
sanctions is an important approach. I was heartened by it,
even though I know it is the exception. We have a lot of
homework to do in the development of political strategies.
We must also attempt to resolve the problems through
changing the law, rather than on a case-by-case basis.

I must admit that part of the problem of inefficient use of
political techniques comes from another aspect of women's
situation. Many women in the traditional community do not
feel beset by any particular problem; they feel satisfied with
the roles and responsibilities that tradition has assigned to
them. Part of our task, then, is to engage women in the
traditional sector, to deal openly and directly with their resistance to changing the status quo. We cannot afford to
ignore them. I have found that sometimes you can scratch
just a little below the surface and the outer shell of resistance
falls away. Women in the traditional sector can be our best
allies in moving the community to come to terms with wom-
en's issues.

We must address the real concerns of the larger community, concerns such as the Jewish family. The family is and
always has been the centerpiece of Jewish life. Yet the family
cannot be used as a cover, a code word for closing off full
access and equality to women in the faith-community. So it

requires of us two things. First, we must put everything out in the open and distinguish between genuine concern for the family (really a concern for Jewish survival) on the one hand, and concern for women's religious growth and spiritual quest on the other. I believe we can somehow get across the message that if a woman opens her mind, it does not necessarily mean she must shut up her womb. Second, we must help the community to build support for women who want to have the best of both worlds, who do not want to be locked into either-or choices. As Jews, we must again be prepared to separate from those elements in society, and in the women's movement, that do not place the family at the center of the concern for equality and the work for equality around that center.

We should applaud and be grateful for signs of change, even small improvements. We should encourage change, and reward those in authority who make changes, those who experiment. Gradual changes should not be put down as imperfect measures. I believe that Jews are continually moving through history toward perfection; and while the Holocaust denies me total assurance that this is so, I still have the faith that we are moving toward messianic times. I don't intend to wait for the Messiah to rectify women's status in Judaism. Rather, I believe that perfection will come as a result of many small things falling into place properly.

Finally, each of us must choose our own style of confrontation, a style that is appropriate to our own psychology, orientation, and talents. I have chosen to do my work largely through lecturing and writing. I am not good at organizing rallies or protests, although I often think that if I could organize a thousand women to protest this or that injustice or limitation, and do it in the right forum, it would have much greater impact than a thousand speeches. And I am not good at creating or leading a moving liturgical experience for women, even though such experiences might do more good than the articles I've written on women and liturgy. But I have to use my strengths as they are, given finite time and energy, and I must be content with my own style of nonconfrontational confrontation. I sometimes try to reassure myself in the face of my deficiencies by telling myself that, through research and writing and lecturing, I am attempting to solve the problem wholesale rather than retail.

These, then, are some of the ideas I've developed as I've moved along. There is, of course, a price one pays for confrontation and change. It goes without saying, however, that you cannot have success without pain, just as you cannot have love without pain. I feel, in fact, that all of this enterprise in the area of women and faith during the last decade has made me grow, not only as a woman but as a Jew. So when the dust settles, and women's equality in traditional Judaism has become very natural, then I'll have my religious surges of the spirit once again. Women have waited a very long time; I can wait a little longer.

3

Change and Confrontation within the Roman Catholic Church

Ann Patrick Ware

Some years ago Alvin Toffler's book *Future Shock* became what its publishers called a "runaway best seller." Toffler described it as a book about "what happens to people when they are overwhelmed by change." The author brilliantly analyzed the disorientation and malaise that many felt because of the greatly accelerated pace of change in our society. He showed what physical and psychic effects we might expect, and he also proposed strategies for survival. Inasmuch as his observations ranged broadly from bioengineering to geriatric communes, from extraterrestrial life to imaginetic centers, from the London Institute for Strategic Studies to Modular Man, I thought it might be of interest to

ANN PATRICK WARE is a Sister of Loretto who currently coordinates the Institute of Women Today, an ecumenical agency assisting incarcerated women. She formerly served as associate director of the Commission on Faith and Order in the National Council of Churches, taught theology at Webster College, and worked in the Justice and Peace Division of Church Women United.

see what he said about the women's movement. Toffler did not mention it. The sole index entry concerning women falls under *Women's Home Companion*, a reference to its having gone out of existence because of television competition!

I relish this chance to reflect on the overwhelming influence of change in the Roman Catholic church in recent years and, in particular, in my own faith-community of the Sisters of Loretto. I relish the chance to reflect also on the underwhelming impact of change—on hopes raised and then thwarted, dreams crafted and then stifled, spirits emboldened and then embittered.

In 1970 there were some 580.5 million Roman Catholics in the world, about 8.5 percent of them in the United States. Approximately one out of four people in the U.S. was a Catholic. Among those 48.2 million U.S. Catholics in 1970 there were close to 60,000 priests; 170,000 sisters; and 12,000 brothers. In 1980, while the total number of Catholics in the U.S. had increased by more than four million, the number of priests had dropped by 2,200; the number of sisters by 52,000; and brothers by 4,500.

Catholics knew three popes in one decade. Paul VI, formerly the popular liberal Cardinal Montini of Milan, carried on the work of the Second Vatican Council begun by his predecessor, but, as he witnessed the profound changes it brought about, he became increasingly tortured, vacillating, lonely, and condemnatory. His successor, John Paul I, was a genial and pious man, doctrinally conservative, whose sudden death shocked the Catholic world as much as did his surprising election. The present pope, John Paul II, is an enigma in many ways; the first non-Italian in modern history, he is also the first pope from the socialist world. Rumor has it that he views the capitalist West as a decadent society and is not likely to be influenced by calls from that world for a rethinking of the church's rigorous stands against the use of artificial contraception, on the prohibition of remarriage after divorce, on mandatory celibacy for the priesthood, and prohibition of the ordination of women. However, like his predecessors, he calls incessantly for disarmament, for justice for the poor, for the rights of workers, for the abolition of capital punishment; and he continues to project an image of a jovial patriarch who has no intention of confining himself to the limits of Vatican City.

Those who stand outside the Catholic fold cannot, I think, understand the symbolic influence of a pope. Even though his words no longer command universal obedience (if ever they did), his voice cannot go unnoticed, especially in time of world crisis or religious upheaval. His dramatic dress, his daily life within the inaccessible Vatican Palace, the archaic and secret workings of the medieval machinery of the pontificate — these provide endless material for speculation. Catholics want to love their pope, having internalized from their earliest years of catechetical instruction the theological understanding that this man was chosen through the intervention of the Holy Spirit, that he is the Vicar of Christ on Earth, that his understanding of the mysteries of faith and the intricacies of God's will is a superior one. To be in the midst of an Italian crowd and to be swept along in the press of bodies amid the frenzied cries of *"Viva!"* and the wild waving of handkerchiefs as the pope appears, stirs even a reserved British heart. A mystique surrounds the papacy and the man who holds it. Thus the short-lived John Paul I, even though he was known to be strongly opposed to feminist concerns within the church, is now quoted fondly in some Catholic feminist circles as the man who said, "God is not only a father but a mother also."

Because of this very real symbolism, the present pope's 1979 visit to the United States was a watershed experience for many of us within the church. We saw this ground-kissing, baby-hugging pope, surrounded by a retinue of men, singing and joking with students, bantering with seminarians, meeting farmers in Iowa, but not once engaged in serious conversation with Catholic women. We learned that the Leadership Conference of Women Religious had tried to arrange an audience with the pope and had failed, and that it was the pope's own wish that none of the eucharistic ministers who served communion at the papal masses be women. We heard the logic: that women could serve only as extraordinary ministers. Masses held outdoors and attended by hundreds of thousands are not extraordinary? We heard the pope stand before the United Nations General Assembly and call for human rights "without discrimination on grounds of origin, race, sex, nationality, religion, political convictions, and the like," and heard him a few hours later telling priests in Philadelphia, to their wild applause, that "the church's traditional decision to call men to the priesthood and not women is not a statement about human rights."

The problem was not that this pope said anything different from the popes before him; it was just that we expected more. This pope is, after all, a poet and philosopher, a playwright, a former member of the underground, a man who wants to be in touch with the contemporary world. He speaks eleven languages, one of which is English, and, as Gabrielle Burton says, because he is a poet we have reason to believe that he chooses words carefully. Yet he speaks of man, men, mankind, brotherhood, sons of God, the history of man and *his* rights, man and *his* heart, man and *his* spirit; he does not speak of womankind, sisterhood, daughters of God, woman and *her* heart, *her* spirit, *her* rights. He uses the feminine only stereotypically: motherland, mother church, mother and queen. Again, as Burton points out, motherland is ruled by males; mother church is ruled by fathers; mother and queen bow to the king; and *m* is for the million times women are invisible in the pope's language.

So when Sister Theresa Kane simply asked, in her speech

of welcome, that the pope "allow the possibility of women as persons being included in all ministries of the church" and that he "be mindful of the intense suffering and pain which is part of the life of many women in these United States," she spoke in her gentle and quiet way for even the more highly radicalized among us. As we watched the events of that visit in 1979, many of us raged and fumed. What we felt was expressed this way by Sister Ritamary Bradley:

Kiss Boy Babies Only . . .

O kiss boy babies only, John Paul Two
Plant purple tenderness on no girl child . . .
Reverse King Herod's rule and let the sword of death descend
Sharp, irreversible upon
Girl children only . . . and cut them off from life . . .
For life flows, as you teach, from bread of Christ
Broken upon the table of the Lord
And shared, in sign of oneness, from the hand
Of those who are his body . . .

Then kiss boy babies only, John Paul Two . . .
And let the girl child grow to nurse and feed
But kiss her not, lest she grow up to feel
That life itself is holy, like the holy bread
That is Christ's broken body . . .
So teach her now, before she can say no
To such a splitting—
That life is holy, life-supplying
Only when the male child, grown to pride
Can feed the hungry, handing out and handling
Christ's very body, which the girl child may not give

Yes, kiss boy babies only, John Paul Two . . .
And push girl babies back with firm command
Blot out the gospel page where Jesus turned unto the
    woman, even in her sin

Against the holding back of Peter and his men ("For shame!
    He speaks there with a woman!")
Let papal lips, empurpled with His blood
Touch no girl babies, only boys.

Blot out the birth story under Bethlehem's stars
Blot out the tomb story where the bloody wounds
Were wiped by women
Blot out the stone story, where the Word
Burst through the stone, and stony hearts,
And kissed with love all those in sight
That Easter day . . . before the dawn
All who were there before the dawn.

The pollsters of the 1970s revealed to Catholics in the
United States that their own system of religious tenets and
practices was undergoing radical change: despite reiteration
of the magisterial teaching on the subject, a majority of
those identifying themselves as Roman Catholic rejected the
church's teaching on the wrongness of artificial contraception; Catholics were getting divorced and remarried in proportion to their demographic density; there was a considera-
ble falling off from obligatory attendance at Sunday Mass;
and Catholic women in significant numbers were undergoing abortion.

In 1974 the Women's Ordination Conference was organized, as was a group calling itself Priests for Equality. Shortly thereafter, a Vatican document appeared, intended to settle once and for all the subject of women's ordination. It
caused a furor because of its untenable theology and interpretation of Scripture, and immediately support for the
ordination of women rose dramatically among Roman Catholics. The increasingly popular liberation theology — import-
ed from Latin American theologians and concerned more
with economic oppression than with sexism — gave biblical
foundation to those who began to see that the church itself

could be oppressive of its members, and the Vatican (where a hundred years is only a moment) made haste to issue a warning about it. Catholics who had grown to think of the catholicity of the church as sameness and immutability were now hard put to understand why some of the very disciplines which they as children had fought against observing and which as adults they were passing on to their children were now optional or, in some cases, even discouraged.

Although I have been a Roman Catholic from the time of my baptism as an infant, I retain scarcely any of the childhood Catholicism that often remains with those individuals who receive a "Catholic education." Instead I became aware of the rich possibilities of religious meaning only as an adult and almost exclusively within a small unit of the church, the Sisters of Loretto. This group of women traces its origins back to the Kentucky frontier in 1812 when a few young women banded together to teach the pioneers' children the rudiments of education, including religion. The settlers were Catholics, having migrated from Maryland, and since there were at the time no public opportunities for education, three young women, rapidly joined by others, undertook to pass on to their young relatives and friends what they had received from the Maryland teachers. We of Loretto like to think that the frontier spirit is ours; that we face change and challenge somewhat as a matter of course; that, not having sprung from some European order with a vastly different history and culture, we are able to adapt more readily to the exigencies of contemporary life here in the United States.

We were never an enormous group, having only eleven hundred members at our largest and in 1980 numbering a little under seven hundred. Our median age was sixty-six; the future of our group, like the future of other canonical congregations within the Roman Catholic church, is uncertain. But we marvel that in the space of fifteen years we moved from a strictly hierarchical structure to one that is collegial and egalitarian. As of 1965, within every religious house of our congregation there was one appointed superior who bore responsibility for the others in the house. Each sister's residence and work were assigned to her, as it were, out of the blue and with no previous consultation. But now sisters choose their work within the context of the community and decide with whom they wish to live. Once we were the recipients of the goods we requested from the superior; now each bears responsibility for budgeting whatever income she has and deciding how she will choose to live the life of simplicity and unclutteredness and sharing to which she has committed herself. In 1965 we gathered several times a day for prayers and other spiritual exercises; today we decide how and when we shall engage in prayer to that God in whose grace we are committed to live the Christian life. In 1965 we were children; now we strive to be independent and interdependent women.

Interestingly enough, these changes came about as a result of a papal directive of the early 1960s that urged religious communities to return to their roots and, in the spirit of their founders, to adapt to the changing world. In my view, the same changes would have come about if the Sisters of Loretto had decided to revise their lives on the basis of feminist principles. A declaration of feminist philosophy would not have been possible for us then, nor is it even possible for us now, but the results are the same. The Loretto community, like the rest of the American populace, is of two minds about feminism: on the one hand, it recognizes the injustices done to women, especially in the economic sphere; on the other hand, it is not certain how much the doctrine of self-fulfillment is to be equated with selfishness or how responsible the women's movement is for some disturbing changes, such as the present transience of relationships, what is perceived as libertine behavior, and a chaotic entry into a new state of affairs whose outcome cannot be imagined.

A record of the Lorettine commitment to women's issues, through the actions of its general assembly during the 1970s, reflects this ambiguity. On the one hand, as early as 1970 we boldly asserted the priority of persons over institutions and made a commitment to detach ourselves from institutions when they no longer give service in the most effective way. This enabled us to move out of places that had obviously served their day — not without great pain but at the same time without denying the value of their past history. This also freed us to undertake new ventures without asking as *the* first question, "How much will it cost?" Instead, viewing money as an institution over which the good of persons has priority, we asked, "What good will it do?" This revolutionary move now meant that we would no longer, for example, send ten sisters to teach at Saint X School without first examining the school to see what caliber of service it provided. And the sisters would no longer be assigned without their consent. Even though we had readily reached accord on this rather bold principle, it was not until 1976 that we saw the connection of our earlier action with the repudiation of patriarchy. We adopted a timidly worded resolution supporting the principle "that women are not meant by God to be subordinate to men, but to be their full equals and partners in the building and sharing of the world." Likewise, in 1974 the Loretto general assembly officially endorsed the Equal Rights Amendment, but in 1979 we had quite a discussion about whether we should officially support an organization called Catholics Act for ERA.

In short, the Loretto community bears within it the same tensions and uncertainties that exist in the country at large. When specific issues of sexism are raised, the Loretto community's reactions are just like reactions elsewhere: denial that the situation exists; trivialization ("How can they be concerned about something so petty?"); false dichotomization ("How can we afford to be concerned about sexism when issues of racism and militarism face us?"); co-optation ("*I've* never experienced any oppression"— generally the reaction of the woman who has "made it" in the male power structure, or of the "token woman"); and above all fear— fear of coming under criticism by men and by women as well, fear of not being liked, fear of setting out on an irreversible path, fear of eventually having to leave the church.

It is clear that changes in the church as well as in society have escalated both the incidence and the intensity of confrontation. Within the Roman Catholic church the main problem is a stark one: How does one get close enough to the people in power to confront them? Women would rather enter into conversation than confrontation, but here we must confess that we Catholic women of opposing views have not even learned how to talk with one another, much less with the male hierarchy. Where we are fortunate enough to evoke a response from the hierarchy, we are left speechless before its assertion that most women are satisfied with their status in the church. We cannot as yet present a unified front on the subjects of the ERA; the use of inclusive language, especially in the liturgy; the painful and tender subject of abortion; the self-determination of religious communities; the ordination of women; and a host of other matters. Only in the rejection of the adamant teaching about artificial contraception does there seem to be a growing agreement, and in the admission by a majority of Catholics that the official Catholic position about divorce and remarriage is harsh.

Beneath these questions lie other issues that have divided the church from its beginning and that have figured in schism throughout its history: How shall decisions be made? What is the value of human experience in determining solutions to problems? What is the nature of the God we worship and how does one know the will of that God? Are there divine laws that never admit exception? Who determines how Scripture shall be interpreted?

Within my religious community the point of confrontation seems to be a clear one: How can one be a Catholic feminist? For those of us who are feminists the case is clear: God is not sexist, but the church — in its institutional structures as well as many of its teachings — is. If we are to be faithful, we must challenge those structures and those teachings at every turn. We are not less Catholic but more Catholic for doing so. For those within my community who disavow the term feminist the case is equally clear: God is known through and is present and active in the Roman Catholic church. God has outfitted the church with an infallible teaching authority, vested primarily in the pope with the college of bishops. Those who do not accept this theological position have no right to call themselves Catholic.

We have not yet learned how to confront one another in positive and growth-producing ways. We are still highly uncomfortable with disagreements because we have traditionally thought it virtuous not to disagree. Thus, in our community we tend:

- to talk on the most serious matters with those who think like us and engage in only superficial conversations with those whom we perceive to hold opposing views;
- to engage in a certain amount of stereotyping; to hide our own opinions behind what others think in phrases like, "I've heard many people say" or "the older sisters think . . .";
- to reduce substantial differences of opinion to a problem in communications, in a phrase like, "we're really saying the same thing";
- to carry on our important disagreements in print, mainly in letters to the editor in our own biweekly community publication, *Interchange*.

From a small community where relationships are intense we may draw some conclusions about confrontation that may apply to the larger feminist society:

- Confrontation is most difficult when one party feels that her opinion is the absolute truth and the other feels that the particular truth under discussion is relative.
- Confrontation is extremely painful when one party gives the other an odious label or denies to the other a quality essential to one's sense of identity or one's integrity. Usually, this is expressed with charges like, "If you think that, you aren't a Christian," or "You're a hypocrite."

A serious question we must reckon with is whether we believe confrontation is *essential* to the healthy growth of a feminist community. I believe that it is. It is a guarantee of our trust in one another that we *can* change and that we care enough for one another to formulate our principles together, in spirit of give and take. For this reason our community favors decision making by consensus.

Our community feels that time is on our side. We have weathered our past disagreements and we have not been pushed into a head-on struggle. If we are so pushed it will be because Rome, through a papal directive, will order us to return to our former way of life: to dress in a certain way, to live under obedience to a superior, to engage only in certain occupations, and so forth — in short, to revert to the childhood we have so recently outgrown. Should this happen, and there are strong indications that it will, it will be a traumatic episode in the life of every community of sisters in this country. Will we survive it?

Here you will excuse me if I offer a tribute to that community of mine, most of whom are well past fifty, as I am myself. We have committed ourselves (and now I quote from our own constitutions) to the principle that the greatest asset of the community is the life of each one of us. We avow that we cannot believe firmly in God's love without trusting human beings, ourselves as well as others. We profess unshakable reliance upon God and human reliance upon one another. We accept the serious and lasting obligation to speak with each other, to listen to each other, and so to be shaped in thought and act. We believe we have come together so that, rejoicing in and strengthened by our mutual love, we may continually go forth to meet our more distant neighbors in their human needs and aspirations. We believe that the Spirit of God is not bound; it reveals itself in the lives of everyone.

We have learned in these days of change and confrontation that we cannot love everyone's ideas, but we are committed to love one another. And that will, please God, carry us through.

4

A Polish-American
Catholic Perspective

Delphine Palkowski

I am a woman of faith reflecting on her Polish heritage, appreciating its rich traditions of culture and faith-life. This heritage has been the foundation of my spirit, and of my ability to love, to share, and to understand others.

Although I have some vague recollections of my early childhood before my father died (he died when I was three and my brother seven years old), I recall primarily my growing-up years in a large three-family house on Detroit's East Side. This was an extended-family environment: upstairs lived my grandparents, two single uncles, and my grandmother's bachelor cousin. My grandparents never had to

DELPHINE PALKOWSKI, a Roman Catholic laywoman, is a founding member of the task force of Women of Faith in the 80s. She has served as administrative director of the Ecumenical Institute for Jewish-Christian Studies in Southfield, Michigan, and as administrative coordinator of the Continuing Professional Education Program at the University of Detroit. Currently a sales representative for the Great Lakes Graphics Publishing Company, she also chairs the advisory board of the Detroit Women's Forum and serves on the subcommittee for Jewish-Christian relations of the archdiocese of Detroit.

learn to speak English. Everyone in the neighborhood and the markets spoke Polish.

In the larger of the downstairs units lived another uncle, his wife, and their two children. One of these cousins, Dolores, is a year older than I; through the years, she has been like a sister to me, and a totally loving, supporting friend.

My mother, brother, and I also lived downstairs, in the smaller front flat. In the afternoons my mother worked in my uncle's bakery. Frequently, I helped out at the bakery after school. The trip entailed two buses each way. One of my assignments at the bakery was to clean the pie pans that were stacked half-way to the ceiling. It seemed a never-ending chore. The good news was that I had my choice of the goodies in the showcases.

My grandmother Babcia was a hard worker and the indomitable force in the family. I recall Babcia's marvelous meals: soups lightly thickened with egg yolks and cream; chicken and duck soups with homemade egg noodles; and pierogi, dumplings filled with cheese, sauerkraut, or meat. Babcia's kitchen did not have a lot of gadgets or appliances. Hundreds of pierogi were hand cut with a glass reserved for that purpose. They rested on lightly floured towels every where — tabletop, sewing machine, and ironing board — waiting to be dunked into large steamy pots of boiling water. The meat for the homemade kiebasa was stuffed into the end of the casing through a hollow bull's horn that came from Poland. Great baking took place in Babcia's half-gas, half-wood burning stove. My services were frequently commandeered.

Dust and dirt had no time to settle in Babcia's house. In fact, anyone whose housekeeping did not meet local standards was subject to ridicule from the neighborhood gossips. Even the neighbors' wash line was scrutinized for any gray tinge.

Nor could crabgrass survive in Babcia's garden: on hands

and knees she dug up all undesirables without the use of insecticides. Even the street in front of the house was hosed daily and swept with a strong broom; this was my grandfather's task, along with watering the lawn — assigned, no doubt, by Babcia, who ruled the roost. Babcia never needed "assertiveness training."

My grandfather Dziadzia was a soft-spoken, gentlemanly fellow with soft wavy gray hair and mustache. As he sat on the backsteps on Monday (wash day) mornings, he allowed me to curl his hair with clothespins. He was a gracious host and loved to play cards with his cronies. On Sunday mornings he went to High Mass wearing an immaculate white shirt, his dark blue suit, and a black derby (or a straw hat in the summer). As he ambled along, I recall his low whistling of some Polish tune.

My grandparents truly loved one another. The upstairs porch had large wooden doors that remained open in the summer, leading to a kind of balcony. There was a long bench where one could sit a night and gaze up at the stars. On summer evenings they frequently sat and held hands, softly conversing. Their faith-life was important to them. They were both prayerful. While my grandmother sometimes criticized the human frailties of priests and nuns, the spiritual dedication of my grandparents to their faith and church was strong.

Belonging to a parish was central to the life of the Polish family. In a study titled *The Polish Peasant in Europe and America: Critiques of Research in the Social Sciences,* Thomas and Znaniecki state,

> The Polish parish is much more than a religious association for common worship under the leadership of a priest. The unique power of the parish in Polish-American life is much greater than even the most conservative peasant community in Poland: It cannot be explained by the predominance of

religious interests . . . .The parish is the old primary community, reorganized and concentrated . . . .As an institutional organization it performs the function which in Poland was performed by both the parish and the commune.

In the parish structure the pastor has administrative power, status, prestige, and influence. He might have one or even several assistants. The sisters who taught in the parish schools were ranked between the subordinate assistants and the laity. As John D. Donovan's study *The Social Structure of the Parish* observes, the nuns were

> directly responsible to the pastor, though held in lesser rank than clergy in the eyes of the Catholic Church. At the same time, the formal expectation of their personal sanctity was of fundamental importance to the teaching or other roles in the parish, and the Church regarded them with a prestige and rank superior to that of the laity.

One of the reasons that Polish parochial schools were so successful, in addition to the cheap labor of the sisters, was that immigrant parents were fearful of losing their influence over their children if they sent them to the public schools. They saw their precious traditions discarded as their children adapted to American society. The necessity of a Polish Catholic education was emphasized to both the parents and children of the parish. In fact, parishioners were led to believe by both priests and nuns that it was sinful not to send one's children to a parochial school.

A negative aspect of the children's attending Polish parochial schools in the early twentieth century was that parents were not encouraged to send their children to college. In *Behold! The Polish American*, Joseph Wytrawl states,

> The Polish pastors were concerned with preserving their authority, while insisting on retaining the Polish customs and

language without simultaneously integrating the children into the American society. They did not stress higher education, and if they had, it was merely in terms of preparing for the religious orders, or skilled trades . . . . The Polish American clergy failed miserably in inculcating the value of higher education into the cautious and thrifty parents of their parishes, still anxious about surviving future economic depressions.

The dedication to the Catholic faith was very strong in my mother, Stella, who was born in 1904. She was the oldest of six, and the only daughter. This meant great involvement with child rearing and household chores. To escape her domineering mother, at seventeen years Stella married a man much older than herself; he was acceptable to her parents since he came from the same area of Poland as they. She was married for twelve years and had two children; after being widowed, she returned to her parents' house to lease one of the flats at fifteen dollars per month.

Stella struggled financially to remain independent and was a very capable woman. Yet she never asserted herself to her mother, not even to the extent of smoking a cigarette in front of Babcia, who did not approve, even though grandfather and uncles also smoked.

Nor did my mother remarry until after Babcia died; by that time, my brother was in the army and I was married and had a home of my own. Mother married Martin, her close friend for over seventeen years. We fondly called him Pops and loved him as a father. He later became an affectionate, doting grandfather, still called Pops by the grandchildren.

Perhaps the attitude inculcated at an early time, that higher education was beyond the means of a working family and unnecessary for a girl, prevailed with my mother during my high-school years. Finances were a problem in our little

nuclear family. In the 1940s and fifties it was socially acceptable for women to work prior to marriage and also after,
until a pregnancy occurred. If you were a Catholic, pregnancy would probably occur shortly after marriage. After
high school, I did secretarial work at a law firm and later for
a department-store executive. When I was sixteen I met Joe
Palkowski, and at eighteen I married him.

We lived with my in-laws for five and a half years. After
our son Michael was born and my mother-in-law offered to
baby-sit, I went back to work, for the County of Wayne in
downtown Detroit.

In 1956 we bought a home in the suburbs; my husband
urged me to stop working in order to have another child. I
complied, bearing five additional children in the following
six years. Joe began a business venture and worked long
hours and was usually not home to participate in child
rearing. It was then that I strove to become the stereotyped
superwoman: wife, mother, housekeeper, cook, baker,
chauffeur, and volunteer in church and civic organizations.
I refer to those as my Gerber Years: "babies [were] my business." Between night feedings for infants and meeting the
many needs of toddlers, there were many years with no more
than four hours of sleep per night, rarely more than two
hours at a time.

It was at that time that I became active in parish work
through the Altar Society. In addition to church cleaning
and ironing albs (a long, loose, linen vestment worn by
priests), I found myself as chairwoman of my neighborhood
guild. Our guild was assigned a large fund-raising project:
this project entailed hosting a card party, a fashion show of
men and women's clothing, and a light dinner. About ten of
us women worked diligently to amass over two hundred door
prizes. Our little group labored several nights to prepare a
parish mailing of several thousand letters and packets of
raffle tickets. The day after the mailing, an angry postmas-

ter notified our pastor that it was illegal to send raffle tickets through the mails. The pastor was embarrassed. I was responsible for the mailing; I was also in the middle of my fourth pregnancy. The postmaster chastised me and threatened a year in prison. The specter of giving birth in a jail cell was most disconcerting!

In spite of the challenges, the event was successful both socially and financially. Wearing a new turquoise maternity dress and suffering from stage fright, I managed the introductions and orchestrated the evening for an audience of over fourteen hundred.

Over the years, we moved four times into larger houses to accommodate our growing family. When my youngest daughter, Mary, entered the first grade, with trepidation I enrolled in a college course. It took eleven years to earn my baccalaureate; I majored in communications, with a minor in business. Currently, I am enrolled in a masters program in Public Administration.

Our three sons and three daughters are now young adults. Both our oldest son, Mike, and oldest daughter, Cathy, took time out of their studies at Michigan State University to perform volunteer work in Israel: this was a wonderful learning experience for them. Our second son, Matthew, is presently in the Marist Novitiate in Cambridge, Massachusetts. Daughter Carla and son Mark are self-employed. Mary is a student and part-time waitress.

As I look back over my life, I realize that my years of volunteer church work led to my involvement in Jewish-Christian relations. This endeavor has become very dear to me. My life has been enriched and supported by warm, loving friendships with my Jewish sisters and brothers.

I believe that God chooses to use us as catalysts; we need only to respond. I believe in being a Woman of Faith: to listen, to speak, to share, and to give sustenance to one another is to respond to God. Our pluralistic society gives us the opportunity to enjoy and participate in each other's cultures. For the past six years, Joe and I have been members of a predominantly black Catholic church. Sacred Heart is located near a former Polish neighborhood on Detroit's East Side. We love the cordiality shared within our Sacred Heart family.

I believe that to be middle aged is to exist in the middle of the life span, that is, to deal with the problems of aging parents simultaneously with the problems of growing children. But the middle position also offers an opportunity to become a link between the generations, to be a living example of caring, to instill values, traditions, and an appreciation of the family's cultural heritage.

Personally, I'm very grateful to be in the third generation of a Polish-American family. It was a privilege to have known the first generation, to have been imbued with their values, their traditions, their native language, and their expressions of politesse and gentility. I also appreciate the struggles of the second generation, the pain they experienced during their assimilation into society, and their feeling that they had to reject their families and cultural heritage in order to be accepted as Americans.

When my husband and I were in Israel, we encountered a number of Polish Jews. Their first question was, "Do you feel you are Polish or American?" At first, this surprised me; I've never considered myself anything but American. It was my grandparents who were Polish. I'm proud of my heritage, just as other Americans are enriched by their cultural backgrounds.

I doubt that my children, the fourth generation, will want or will be able to hand on Polish traditions to their families. They've grown up in integrated suburbs. Their ethnic identity is already diminished. However, they do enjoy the holiday traditions with their older relatives and readily participate in the sharing of the "Oplatek" at Christmas and the "Blessed Egg" at Easter. Although they are totally assimilated into American culture, I hope that they will retain a high regard for their ethnic heritage.

My research in sociology and ethnic studies has shown me that we must be sensitive to the needs of newer immigrants to our country. In the Detroit area, we have many Arabs and Chaldeans. There are more Arabic-speaking people in the Detroit area than in any city in the United States. In other cities there has been an influx of Orientals and Latin Americans. As Americans, we should be open and sensitive to their customs and accept them as sisters and brothers so that they do not experience the alienation of earlier immigrants. The lesson we should have learned by now is that they and their children should not be forced to reject their heritage in order to be assimilated into American society.

I conclude by sharing a Polish blessing:

> May your heart be as patient as the earth,
>   Your love as warm as harvest gold.
> May your days be full as the city is full,
>   Your nights as joyful as dancers.
> May your arms be as welcoming as home.
>   May your faith be as enduring as God's love,
> Your spirit as valiant as your heritage.
>   May your hand be as sure as a friend,
> Your dreams as hopeful as a child.
>   May your soul be as brave as your people,
> And may you be blessed with peace.

5

An Asian-American Woman
Reflects on
Racism, Classism, and Sexism

Naomi P. F. Southard

As I approach the task of discussing racism, classism, and sexism, my immediate reaction is to say that they are all alive and well! Despite years of hard work for change, there are still far too many signs of these divisions.

As an Asian-American, I can attest to the presence of these ills as my community strives for reform of immigration laws, adequate health care, housing, full employment, and bilingual education. In the media, there are almost daily instances of denigrating stereotypes of persons of Asian heritage.

Even more disturbing are the signs of complete disregard for Pacific and Asian life: the testing of nuclear weapons in inhabited Pacific areas, human-rights violations in the lands

The REVEREND NAOMI P. F. SOUTHARD is executive director of the National Federation of Asian-American United Methodists. She formerly served as associate general secretary of the Commission on Christian Unity and Interreligious Concerns of the United Methodist Church.

of our Asian heritage, and the increase in acts of racially motivated violence in the United States.

The murder of Vincent Chin is a recent example of the violence we face. Chin, a Chinese-American, was beaten to death by several white auto workers who mistakenly assumed he was Japanese and blamed him for their unemployment. The auto workers were convicted of manslaughter and sentenced to only three years' imprisonment and a fine of three-thousand dollars. The Asian-American community organized in protest against this unjustly light sentence, and the killers were indicted a second time for violating Chin's civil rights. One of the men was acquitted of this charge and another was convicted; he is currently appealing that decision.

Vincent Chin's murder is both a symbol and frightening example of the combined forces of economic decline and racism. The virulence of classism, racism, and sexism has often been felt in periods of economic hardship — and it is likely to grow more intense in the days ahead, as the middle class and the working poor find it increasingly difficult to meet their basic survival needs.

In the face of this rather depressing forecast, I can only say that I have not given up. I cannot give up, for several reasons: first, because of my conscience and my calling as a woman of faith; second, because of my survival as a member of a minority group in the United States; and third, because of my integrity and, I believe, the very state of my soul as a member of a privileged class in a world with so much hunger and poverty. I say for myself, "I have not given up." You must not give up, either, for I cannot go on alone.

Our task is one of transformation. Sexism, classism, and racism have in common the assumption that persons of one group (be it class, race, orientation, or gender) can justifiably control or otherwise dominate persons not in their group. If we are to go on together in the work of transforming the system so that all may equitably share in the blessings of this earth, we must begin with personal transformation. We must be transformed from persons of loss to persons of vision.

For me, this personal transformation finds its primary source and meaning in my community. It is in recalling the past that the key to transformation lies. Although it is filled with bitter experiences, the past is also a chronicle of survival.

This chronicle begins with my grandmother. Yukino Yoshino Tashiro lived through the loss of homeland and family, and suffered years of poverty, overwork, and discrimination. At the age of eighteen she left her parents, siblings, and aspirations for a teaching career in order to fulfill her first duty, marriage. She still recalls two weeks of seasickness as she accompanied her new husband to an alien land, not knowing if she would ever see Japan again. The laws of this new country, which welcomed her enthusiastically as a worker, denied her the right to become a citizen or to own land.

Like other Issei (first generation Japanese-American) women, she worked a full day—at manual labor in a fruit field, as a storekeeper, and later as a domestic servant—while she bore primary responsibility as a caretaker of a home and eleven children.

Historian Emma Gee quotes a woman of my grandmother's generation:

My husband was a Meiji man. He did not think of helping me in the house or with the children. No matter how busy I may have been, he never changed the babies' diapers. Though it may not be right to say it ourselves, we Issei pioneer women from Japan worked solely for our husband. At mealtime, whenever there was not enough food, we served a lot to our husbands and took little for ourselves.[1]

There were certainly days when my grandmother questioned how and whether she could go on. And yet, on the occasions when she told me her history, I never heard an undertone of complaint. She and others of her generation lived by a motto that grows out of our Japanese Buddhist heritage: *shikata ga nai*. It means, "there's nothing that can be done"; hardship is a natural part of life; it will be endured without complaint. While her life might easily have been full of bitterness, she claimed a transforming power in her faith and will to survive. *Shikata ga nai*, watchword of her religion and culture, enabled her to withstand racism, sexism, and classism.

My grandmother's strength was an important legacy to her Nisei (second generation) children. My mother, Sumiko Tashiro Southard, and more than 110,000 persons of Japanese ancestry (many of whom were United States citizens) were interned from 1942 to 1946. The campaign of racist hate that led to the imprisonment of virtually all Japanese-Americans on the West Coast was waged in many cases by persons who were jealous of the agricultural and business successes of Japanese-Americans.

The campaign was swift and successful. A little more than two months after the bombing of Pearl Harbor, the United States declared war against Japan and, with the signing of Executive Order 9066, authorized the evacuation of Japanese-Americans from designated "military areas." One month later, the first group of three thousand people was removed to the Assembly Center at Santa Anita, California. During this period, violence and fear pervaded the Japanese-American community. Young children were spit at and called names; a Niesi friend recalls hanging blankets on the windows to block bullets fired at their home. In southern California there were a series of attacks on Japanese residents, some of which were fatal. Wartime panic was directed against the innocent, simply because of their race. There never has been any evidence whatsoever that Japanese-Americans were involved in espionage or other acts of disloyalty to the United States: they were suspected only of aiding the enemy and of being "unassimilable." In an attempt to demonstrate their loyalty to the United States, the overwhelming majority of Japanese-Americans chose not to resist removal and incarceration, while many of the young men volunteered to join the armed services.

My family was rounded up and taken to the Amache Relocation Center in the isolated southeastern desert of Colorado to await an unknown fate. Michi Nishiura Weglyn, an internee, sums up those "years of infamy":

> Since the first shock of the Pearl Harbor attack, the Nisei, by being lumped in with aliens as "non-aliens" (to obscure the fact of their citizenship) had endured every possible humiliation. They had been bombarded by press denunciations. They had been crucified on the lie that they were more suspect than their alien parents, rejected in their efforts to volunteer for the armed services, stripped of their rights as citizens.[2]

Dehumanizing conditions in the camps resulted in suicide, chronic depression, aggravated illness, the breakdown of family bonds, and the loss of identity through the enforced denial of Japanese heritage.

The social isolation and injustice of the war years has had profound psychic repercussions among the Nisei; according to Weglyn, there is a

> deep consciousness of personal inferiority, a proclivity to noncommunication in inarticulateness, evidenced in a shying away from exposure which might subject them to further hurt. This behavior was summed up by Nisei activist Edison Uno: "We were like the victims of rape. We felt shamed. We could not bear to speak of the assault."[3]

While there is pain (much of it silent) regarding the war-time internment, there is little bitterness. The Japanese-American community has persevered in addressing the violation of civil and human rights involved in the removal. In 1976, President Ford rescinded Executive Order 9066. However, despite a full government investigation of the spurious justifications for the internment, there has not been an apology from the United States government to our community. At present, several Japanese-American organizations have filed appeals to press the question of appropriate redress and reparations. Although we have had little success in bringing the matter to Court, we are continuing our efforts to ensure that this injustice will neither be forgotten nor repeated against others.

The oppressiveness of camp life and the prospect of returning virtually penniless to an "outside" society that was overcome with anti-Japanese fever did not deter my mother from making her way to Chicago with a younger sister. There she earned a living and was able to help the rest of the family settle in a home in San Francisco at the end of the war. When I look to her experience for an understanding of how to go on in the face of rejection and severe discrimination, I see in her an unshakable spirit of patient persistence. Whatever the obstacles in her way, she moved ahead one step at a time, looking for each opportunity to provide security for her family. Throughout her youth and eventually as a young widowed mother, she worked full-time and helped with the care and education of her younger siblings and, later, her daughter. She made many sacrifices — going without a badly needed coat or spending late hours making clothes for her family. Her legacy to me is the knowledge that one goes on not only for oneself, but also for the sake of the family and the community. When I feel overwhelmed by the enormity of racism, sexism, and classism, I find strength in her example. If I give up, others will not be able to continue. We learn daily new ways in which all of us are part of the same community; we must go on together because our fates are inseparable.

In the heritage I have outlined thus far, we cannot forget the greatest suffering experienced by persons of Japanese ancestry — that of those who suffered the atomic bomb. The only people who have been victims of the most dreaded form of aggression we know — of nuclear attack — are my family, my people, people of color.

I define my own place in this heritage as a biracial woman. All my life I have been plagued with the arrogant question "What are you?" — as though my race and identity were anybody's business but my own. I was never allowed to sidestep the question, for people persisted until they could place me in a racial category. Inquiries made by teachers, playmates, and even strangers on the street clearly indicated that my race was disturbing and problematic. At an early age I was aware that many people looked upon interracial marriage with horror. My "mixed blood" was for many people more significant than my character.

As a young female, I was expected by Asians and non-Asians alike to conform to stereotypical behavior. Virtually everyone I encountered stood in authority over me, and it was my role to agree and obey. Although my family wanted me to do well in school, there was never an expectation that I would amount to much professionally. I was praised only when I was docile and quiet. My worth, I thought, depended upon my submissiveness.

Economic times were not easy when I was growing up in my extended family. My mother found a way to enroll me in a school in a middle-class neighborhood to avoid the lower educational standards of the schools near our home. Because of my race and the neighborhood in which I lived, few children at school were allowed by their parents to visit my home. Considerations of race and class impinged on even the simplest daily events. When I was going to a toy store to find out if a piece of dollhouse furniture was the right size, my mother warned me not to bring a tape measure because the proprietor might think I had stolen it. I did not question why he would come to that conclusion; I accepted that there was something about me that might justify suspicion.

The stigma and consequences of prejudice pursue us, from daily interactions between children to the ultimate destructiveness of war. I turn to my adopted Christian tradition for an image of the new community which can reinforce my resolve to go on in the face of racism, sexism, and classism. One of the many biblical passages that suggests to me how the harmony of creation can be experienced is in the Gospel according to John, chapter 14. There Jesus tells the ones he loves of a house that has many rooms: "If it were not so, would I go to prepare a place for you? And when I go to prepare a place for you, I will come again and will take you to myself, that where I am, you may be also."

The careful preparation of this house brings to mind the thoughtful plans made for a cherished and long-awaited guest. It speaks to me of an awareness and a care for the guest's every need. This concern grows from a love that desires to comfort and to be intimately present with the guest. The guest would feel like one of the family, never wanting— or being asked—to leave.

In the new house, the new community, you will need no immigration papers to enter; you will have a space of your own and will be accepted for what you are. Persons of every color, age, gender, social status, physical and emotional condition, and sexual orientation will have a place. The goal of our existence would be to remain in harmony with one another and with God.

This idealistic vision of community is a source of renewal for me when I must persevere against hostile institutional powers. It strengthens me when I am faced with the anger of my Asian brothers for my independent and assertive behavior; or with their jealousy when I am rewarded for professional efforts. I need to be reminded of an ideal goal when my loyalties, energies, and commitments are claimed by an overwhelming number of worthy causes: ethnic groups, women, peace, justice, hunger, and others.

I return also to these words of Cherrie Moraga:

> The vision of our spirituality provides us with no trapdoor solution, no escape hatch tempting us to "transcend" our struggle. We must act in the everyday world. Words are not enough. We must perform visible and public acts that may make us more vulnerable to the very oppressions we are fighting against.[4]

I have expressed my vision in Christian terms, but I know that we all share a history of great strength of faith that transcends the limits of our particular communities and personal identities. I have shared my history of transformation not because it is unusual, but because it bears so many similarities to the stories of immigrant Americans past and present. My own profession of faith is anchored in several ways: I cling to the adventurous and indomitable spirit of my Buddhist grandmother; I am grateful for the nurture and self-giving of my Buddhist-Christian mother; and now I look to the support, wisdom, and love of my Jewish, Muslim, and other sisters of faith as we seek together to build a new community in which power and powerlessness are reunited.

Each of us has a story to tell of how the forces of racism, sexism, classism — and the forces of faith, sacrifice, and persistence — have shaped our lives. I ask you to continue to share these stories with each other. As we tell each other of the injustices that have invaded our memories we will be led again to the inevitable conclusion that transformation *should* take place. Recounting the chronicle of our survival will remind us that transformation *will* take place. Because someone or something has called us here, we can be bearers of the new community. There is a constant need to relate our inspiration to our task. In the words of Afro-Cuban feminist Luisah Teish:

> Coming into spirituality the way I did, changed the Christian myth that there is nothing we can do — we are totally powerless. I found that when there was trouble, my people did not say "Okay, we can't fight, we just have to let God handle it." They went and made sacrifices, they evoked their Gods and Goddesses, and they went out there and fought. You learn to take power when there is a presence behind you.[5]

NOTES

1. Emma Gee, "Issei Women: 'Picture Brides' in America," in *Immigrant Women*, ed. Maxine Schwartz Seller (Philadelphia: Temple University Press,) p. 59.

2. Michi Nishiura Weglyn, *Years of Infamy*. (New York: Morrow Quill Paperbacks, 1976), p. 135.

3. Ibid., p. 273.

4. Cherrie Moraga and Gloria Anzaldua, eds., *This Bridge Called My Back: Writings by Radical Women of Color*. (Watertown, MA: Persephone Press, 1981), p. 195.

5. Ibid., p. 296.

6

An Evangelical Perspective on Interreligious Dialogue

Virginia Ramey Mollenkott

Because authentic dialogue can take place only when participants start from a clearly defined sense of who they are, I
shall begin with a brief definition of my own religious stance
an an evangelical. With several modifications, I can affirm
Marvin R. Wilson's definition of an evangelical as "a Christian who believes, lives, and desires to share the Gospel." The
modifications are that one must allow for some latitude in
defining the Gospel (or "Good News"), and that one must
stress Wilson's later statement that the "formal principle" for
separating evangelicalism from other Protestant movements
is the doctrinal issue of biblical authority. Wilson is correct
that

DR. VIRGINIA RAMEY MOLLENKOTT is professor of English at The William
Paterson College of New Jersey. She is the author of nine books and many
articles on literary, pedagogical, theological, and feminist topics. A lifetime member of the Evangelical Women's Caucus, she served as a stylistic
consultant for the New International Version of the Bible and was a
member of the National Council of Churches committee that prepared
An Inclusive Language Lectionary: Readings for Years A, B, and C.

within contemporary evangelicalism there remains an overall consensus of belief in the complete reliability and trust-
worthiness of Scripture and a corresponding conviction that
Scripture stands as the final authority in matters of faith and
practice.[1]

For this reason, my approach to interreligious issues will
focus very closely on the Bible.

Within evangelicalism, I locate myself on the radical left.
In *Essentials of Evangelical Theology*, Donald G. Bloesch
congratulates the evangelical left for its "well-meaning attempts to relate the Gospel to the social arena," but has
criticized us for tending at times to "lose sight of the transcendent dimensions of the Gospel message and for too easily
aligning Christianity with radicalism."[2] Professor Bloesch's
only illustration of too-easy alignment of Christianity with
radicalism is my statement that the Bible, interpreted con-
textually, supports the central tenets of the feminist movement. I am often the target of such attacks from more conservative evangelicals; and I admit this at the outset so that
people are forewarned not to consider my views typical of
evangelicalism as a whole. However, Bloesch has in fact
wrenched my statement on feminism out of its context. Because I agree that the Gospel "must not be reduced [exclu-
sively] to a political theology," and because I do hold a strong
view of biblical authority, I still classify myself as an evangelical.

Evangelicals of the right are properly spoken of as fundamentalists. Recently many American fundamentalists have
organized politically as part of the New Right. Their power
has been evident in recent national elections. But prior to
their recent flurry of repressive political activity, fundamentalists emphasized individual salvation and a privatized ethic to such a degree that they virtually ignored community
responsibility.[3]

Partly to counterbalance my own early fundamentalist training, I now place great stress on the liberating implications of the Gospel. Through a long spiritual evolution I have become convinced that the *evangelium*, the Good News, is biblically intended to be Good News to all the oppressed and wretched of the earth by turning people of faith into agents of peace and justice. True to my evangelical roots, I have found that the Bible itself has been my chief radicalizer. It seems to me that, according to Scripture, a *central* sign of God's Spirit-filled servant is refusal to withdraw from the struggle to establish justice on earth (see especially Isaiah 42:1–4).

Because the fundamentalist viewpoint makes little distinction between witnessing or evangelizing and proselytizing, there is very little hope of drawing fundamentalists into formal interreligious dialogue. The best advice I can offer to people who are disturbed by fundamentalist attempts to proselytize is to publicize broadly and repeatedly the distinctions between psychological manipulation, materialistic inducement, and unethical coercion on the one hand, and simple communication of the facts of one's spiritual journey on the other.[4] Interreligious dialogue is possible only as people quietly and realistically describe their religious experience, giving their reasons for the faith that is in them, while at the same time seeking to understand and appreciate religious experience from other points of view. Like other people, some evangelicals may be drawn to see that there is no sense trying to force agreement concerning external religious forms; like other diversities, these would appear to exist with the permission of God. But we *can* talk, and talk meaningfully, about the inner spiritual essence that is expressed through external religious forms. And we can do it without casting aspersions on any particular form and without disloyalty to the form that is deeply meaningful to us.[5] We can attempt, through our dialogue, to find practical ways to overcome some of the divisive attitudes and actions caused by parochial devotion to our own tradition without awareness of the ultimate unity behind all religious traditions. In a far deeper sense than many of us perhaps can realize, "the LORD our God, the LORD is one" (Deuteronomy 6:4) and "There is one body and one Spirit . . . one [Sovereign], one faith, one baptism; one God and . . . [Parent] of all, who is over all and through all and in all" (Ephesians 4:4–5, inclusive language mine).

Perhaps the best way to draw evangelicals into interreligious dialogue is through emphasis on the precedent provided in the Book of Books, and particularly through pointing out a biblical theme that has not been widely proclaimed in evangelical circles: namely, the theme of universal salvation. So underplayed is this biblical theme among evangelicals that Bloesch lists it among the heresies that pose a threat to Christianity.[6] However, I agree with John Milton that no position should be termed heretical unless it has been arrived at in defiance of the Bible.[7]

For the purposes of stimulating interreligious dialogue, a helpful and precedent-setting focus would be the *biblical basis* of universal redemption. This theme runs like a scarlet thread of hope through both the Hebrew and Christian Scriptures. Since most evangelicals accord equal importance to the Hebrew and Christian Scriptures, what we term Old Testament evidence[8] is just as important as that which is drawn from the New Testament.[9] But of course it would be helpful to focus on those passages that show a close similarity between Hebrew and Christian forms—especially in order to allay the fears of those evangelicals who think that to affirm universalism is to render unavailing the life and passion of Jesus. (I focus on allaying *evangelical* fears because universalism poses less of a problem for more liberal Christians and for Jewish people).

For instance, it might be helpful to evangelicals to be

reminded that the very Psalm Jesus echoed on the cross, Psalm 22, does not stop at its heart-wringing cry of abandonment but goes on to a powerful affirmation of universal redemption:

> All the ends of the earth
> will remember and turn to the LORD,
> and all the families of the nations
> will bow down before . . . [God].[10]

Another important connection might be the one between Isaiah 45:23 and Philippians 2:10–11. Clearly the Philippians hymn adapts Isaiah's vision that "Before me every knee will bow;/ by me every tongue will swear." Although the difference between Jew and Christian is underlined by the fact that the Philippians Epistle says it is "at the name of Jesus" that every knee will bow, it will be news to most evangelicals that the climactic Adoration Prayer recited in the synagogue reads: "Fervently we pray that the day may come . . . when all who dwell on earth shall know that to Thee alone every knee must bend and every tongue give homage."[11]

To mitigate evangelical exclusivism, another particularly helpful passage might be Matthew 8:11: Jesus' echo of Isaiah's prophecies that people of all nations would return to the God of Israel. When Jesus was asked by a Roman soldier to heal his beloved servant-boy, Jesus marveled at the soldier's faith and commented that "many will come from the east and the west, and will take their places at the feast with Abraham, Isaac, and Jacob in the kingdom of heaven." Thus Jesus confirmed the universal outreach of the vision of Isaiah and other Hebrew prophets, making that intention explicit by responding enthusiastically to the faith of an "outsider," a Roman soldier. As for our Muslim sisters and brothers, we need only remind ourselves of God's tender concern for outcast Hagar and Ishmael, as recorded in Genesis 21:8–21. Some evangelicals might be stimulated to respectful dialogue with people of Islamic religion by being reminded that God was indeed *with Ishmael* and has fulfilled the divine promise to make of Ishmael a mighty nation.

Evangelical dialogue with people of other religions may also be facilitated by lifting up a second and closely related biblical theme: the concept that faithfully attempting to serve truth and justice to the best of one's understanding will lead to salvation. Here again, evangelicals are more disturbed than most others might be, because evangelicals are trained to equate the Gospel with our own tradition's understanding of it, which in turn is assumed to be the clear Word of God for everyone. Inevitably, such training causes confusion between God's truth and a particular point of view on almost any topic.

One way to alleviate evangelical anxiety may be to stress Jesus' statement about the *inscrutable* workings of God's Spirit: "The wind blows wherever it pleases. You hear its sound, but you cannot tell where it comes from or where it is going. So it is with everyone born of the Spirit" (John 3:8). Another way may be to ask consideration of the fact that, expanding upon Moses, Jesus asserted flatly that eternal life depends on love of God and neighbor (Luke 10:25–28; cf. Deuteronomy 6:5 and Leviticus 19:18). We can also point out that in John 10:10 the Good Shepherd is portrayed as saying, "I have other sheep that are not of this sheep pen. I must bring them also. They will listen to my voice, and there shall be one flock and one shepherd"; and that 1 Timothy 2:3 stimulates faith in the thoroughness of God's redemptive outreach by assuring us that "God our Savior . . . wants all . . . [people] to be saved and to come to a knowledge of the truth" (inclusive language mine).

As Malachi pointed out (1:11), God promises that "My name will be great among the nations, from the rising to the setting of the sun. In every place incense and pure offerings will be brought to my name . . . ." Paul upheld Malachi's vision by remarking that even though the Athenians were worshiping God ignorantly, they were indeed worshiping *God* (Acts 17:22–23).

Although Hebrew prophets describe universal salvation as a return to the God of Israel, and Christian prophets look toward the bringing of all things under the control of the Christ, their underlying agreement about the New Creation is unmistakable: peace and mutuality under God's gracious rule, the lion and the lamb lying down together. And as we have seen, some prophets from both Judaism and Christianity have specifically envisioned a redemption that reaches to people of faith beyond the confines of their own tradition. Their vision seems to me a good paradigm for interreligious dialogue: each of us maintaining loyalty to the external forms of our own religion, yet willing to share an inner experience and universal outreach with people whose external forms differ significantly from our own. Although each of us may secretly nourish the expectation that when the Day of God is fully revealed, everyone else will be brought into the fold we ourselves already inhabit, fortunately this is not a matter that has to be settled while we are sharers together of the ambiguous human condition. Like Abraham who pleaded with God for the lives of strangers he had never even seen (Genesis 18:25), we can trust that the Judge of all the earth will do right.

Thus far I have been attempting to share my understanding of evangelical and fundamentalist exclusivism, the chief deterrent to dialogue with people of other religious views. I have also offered a few suggestions about how to attempt to leap over the exclusivist hurdle. Let me turn now to a few issues I believe to be urgent for a coalition of women of faith. What I have to say boils down to the implementation of the familiar vision of the "new humanity" offered in Galatians

3:28: a new humanity in which the exclusionary barriers of race, sex, and economic status have melted, since there is said to be no more Jew or Greek, no slave or free, no male or female. I see the Book of Ruth as a Hebrew paradigm of the same vision, since from being racially an outsider, Ruth went on to become a member of King David's bloodline; from being in poverty, she was welcomed to glean the fields of Boaz and was later more fully provided for in marriage; and from being a mere woman in a sexist society, she was finally acclaimed as better to Naomi than seven sons.

Let me say a few words about the current challenges to those of us who would like to implement the new humanity. With the recent resurgence of the Ku Klux Klan and the Nazi party within our national boundaries, women of faith in the United States cannot afford to keep silent about the biblical vision of a new humanity that crushes the serpentine head of racism. Back in 1963, at the Chicago Conference on Religion and Race, Protestant, Roman Catholic, and Jewish leaders agreed that racial discrimination violates our common understanding of human creation in the image of God. Yet more than twenty years later, justice for America's racial minorities is far from achieved, and indeed some recent gains are rapidly being eroded. At the 1980 Detroit Conference on Theology in the Americas, women of color requested conversation and cooperation with white women only on the condition that we whites begin to pay serious attention to our own racism. *White* racism! Since from the standpoint of the global village we whites are the minority group, for our own sake it is high time that we set our racial attitudes in order.

Just as prejudice toward people of color is a white problem, anti-Semitism is a *Christian* problem. Yet "the church in the practice of anti-Semitism rejects the nation of God's election, and in doing so, (at a very deep level) rejects the Gospel," since according to John 4:22, "salvation is from the

Jews."[12] Because anti-Semitic bias is a Christian problem, we Christians ought to train our minds to recognize and combat it.

As for sexism, we women of faith have our work cut out for us. The very structures of most national religious organizations continue to reflect a profoundly alienating sexism, with fundamentalist and evangelical church structures the most sexist of all. The prophet Joel proclaimed that in the "Day of the Lord," God would pour out the divine Spirit upon *all* people so that both sons and daughters would prophesy; and even on *all* God's servants, both men and women, God would pour out the spirit (Joel 2:28–29). At Pentecost, the Apostle Peter claimed that the Christian church was experiencing the fulfillment of Joel's prophecy (Acts 2:16–18). Yet despite such biblical hints of God's ultimately inclusive intention, neither in Judaism nor in Christianity do we see women fully incorporated as first-class citizens.

To treat its members equally, an organization must not exclude candidates from its offices on the basis of gender or any other factor those candidates did not choose and cannot change. People must be screened for office not on the basis of such categories, but on their individual qualifications. Otherwise, regardless of pious rationalizations, their personhood has been denied. So it stands to reason that were the various religious denominations really devoted to human equality, women would be represented at every level of leadership *in proportion to our numbers in the pews.* Anything less than first-class citizenship represents a structural, institutional denial that women as well as men were made in God's image and given coresponsibility for the remainder of the creation, as Genesis clearly affirms (1:27–28).

I cannot leave the subject of sexism without asking our coalition of women of faith to work toward overcoming heterosexist cruelty toward sexual minorities. At the previously mentioned Conference on Theology in the Americas, for several days more than six hundred liberation-oriented radical church people had nothing to say about discrimination against and persecution of gay and lesbian people. The issue remained, as it so often does, invisible and untouchable until eight embattled women and men got together to prepare a plea for justice to homosexuals. Here again, as opposed to exclusion by category, ordination for the individually qualified person is the hallmark of respect for human personhood.

Hershel Matt has cogently argued that

> even the role of rabbi should be open to a homosexual *if* he or she honestly holds the conviction — and would conscientiously seek to convey it to others — that, in spite of his or her homosexuality, the Jewish ideal for men and women is heterosexuality.

Matt continues, "After all, it is accepted that a single or divorced person can legitimately and effectively serve as rabbi provided that he or she holds up marriage as the [Jewish] ideal."[13] Such sweet reason is urgently needed in every religious tradition here represented, but I doubt it will be heard if we women lack the courage to give it voice.

Historian John Boswell has shown us that Christianity's intolerance toward homosexuals did not become pronounced until the thirteenth century and was paralleled by increased intolerance toward heretics, Jews, and Muslims.[14] Historically, therefore, our cause is a common one: minority persons must all hang together or surely we will all hang separately.

Finally, the biblical vision of the new humanity calls us to work toward economic justice in a world of ever increasing inequities. One Sabbath Day in a Galilean synagogue, Jesus read from Isaiah 61:1–2. And as E. Stanley Jones pointed out, the passage Jesus chose that day beautifully sets forth a program for modern people of faith: to proclaim

> good news to the poor (that is, the economically disinherited) . . . release to the captives (the socially and politically disinherited) . . . recovery of sight to the blind (the physically disinherited) . . . to set at liberty those who are oppressed (the morally and spiritually disinherited) . . . to proclaim the acceptable year of the Lord (a new beginning on a world scale).[15]

The biblical thrust toward equitable distribution of resources is amply illustrated by the ancient institution of the Year of Jubilee (Leviticus 25:8–17, 23–24). Since property was to revert to its original owner every fiftieth year, obviously the point was to prevent the accumulation of wealth in the hands of the few. In a world of multinational corporations that continually widen the gap between the many who hunger and the few who wallow in opulence, we women of faith must struggle for distributive justice. We cannot allow ourselves to forget Isaiah's pronouncement of woe on those who "add house to house/ and join field to field/ till no space is left/ and you live alone in the land" (5:8).

All that I have been saying can of course be subsumed under the single plea that we women of faith join forces to overcome the "us versus them" mentality that may yet doom our world to nuclear destruction. Human beings seem driven to separate the human race into two groups—capitalist versus communist, male versus female, black versus white, Christian versus non-Christian, good versus evil, and so forth—but all our divisions are ultimately variations on the theme of us versus them. And inevitably we forget that "we are they to them as they are them to us,"[16] so that *all* will either live together or die together. By our living and loving, may we manifest the fact that, at the most significant of all levels, we are *not* "us versus them" because in our diversity we are all the one offspring of God. As such, we are intended to embody God's new humanity. And in that joyous faith, may we go from strength to strength.

NOTES

1. "An Evangelical Perspective on Judaism" in *Evangelicals and Jews in Conversation on Scripture, Theology, and History*, ed. Marc H. Tanenbum, Marvin H. Wilson, and A. James Rudin (Grand Rapids: Baker Book House, 1978), pp. 4, 6.

2. Vol. 1 (New York: Harper and Row, 1978), pp. 3, 6.

3. See Carl F. H. Henry, *The Uneasy Conscience of Modern Fundamentalism* (Grand Rapids: Eerdmans, 1947), and *Plea for Evangelical Demonstration* (Grand Rapids: Baker Book House, 1971). As mentioned, recent fundamentalist efforts seem to be moving toward a repressive civil religion through such political pressure groups as Moral Majority and Christian Voice.

4. For support from an evangelical source, see Donald Tinder's article on the ethical aspects of evangelism in *Baker's Dictionary of Christian Ethics*, ed. Carl F. H. Henry (N.P.: Canon Press, 1973), p. 225.

5. See Frithjof Schuon, *The Transcendent Unity of Religions*, rev. ed. (New York: Harper and Row, 1975).

6. *Essentials of Evangelical Theology*, vol. 1, pp. 18–19.

7. "Of True Religion, Heresy, Schism, Toleration," in *The Student's Milton*, ed. Frank Allen Patterson (New York: Appleton-Century Crofts, 1961), pp. 914–19.

8. Among Old Testament universalist passages are the following: Ps. 47; Isa. 2:2–5, 11:1–9, 12, 45:22–23, 60:1–3, 66:22–23; Ezek. 34:23; Hos. 2:18–23; Zeph. 3:9; Zech. 14:9; Mal. 1:11.

9. Among New Testament universalist passages are the following: Matt. 8:10–12; John 10–16; 1 Cor. 15:22; Ephesians 1:9–10; Phil. 2:5–13; Colossians 1:20.

10. Verse 27, NIV. All Bible quotations are from the New International Version, prepared by a team of evangelical scholars (Grand Rapids: Zondervan Bible Publishers, 1978). Out of respect for Jewish usage, I have retained the term LORD, though I prefer the common-gender term Sov-

ereign. However, because of my belief that exclusively masculine language concerning God weakens the self-esteem of women and thus adds to our oppression, here and elsewhere I have repeated the word *God* rather than utilizing a masculine singular pronoun. I have also substituted inclusive language whenever the usage seems to exclude women from membership in God's human family.

11. *The Bible Reader: An Interfaith Interpretation*, ed. Walter M. Abbott, S. J.; Rabbi Arthur Gilbert; Rolfe Lanier Hunt; and J. Carter Swaim (New York: Bruce Books, 1969), p. 441.

12. James Daane, *The Anatomy of Anti-Semitism and Other Essays on Religion and Race* (Grand Rapids, Eerdmans, 1965), pp. 30–31.

13. "Sin, Crime, Sickness or Alternative Life Style: A Jewish Approach to Homosexuality," in *Homosexuality and Ethics*, ed. Edward Batchelor, Jr. (New York: The Pilgrim Press, 1980), p. 124. For an evangelical perspective, see Letha Scanzoni and Virginia Ramey Mollenkott, *Is the Homosexual My Neighbor? Another Christian View* (New York: Harper and Row, 1978).

14. *Gay People in Western Europe from the Beginning of the Christian Era to the Fourteenth Century* (Chicago: University of Chicago Press, 1980).

15. *The Bible Reader*, p. 735.

16. R. D. Laing, "Us and Them," in *The Writer's World*, ed. George Arms, William M. Gibson, and Louis G. Locke (New York: St. Martin's Press, 1978), p. 80.

PART TWO

A Dialogue concerning
Our Struggles within Our Own
Religious Communities

Roman Catholic scholar Rosemary Radford Ruether leads off this dialogue with an analysis of the pathologies of sexism, and of women's liberation as a witness to a new humanity, with major focus on the suppression of women within Christianity. Next, Lutheran Mary L. Chrichlow describes her struggles as a black woman in a racist and sexist society, and her work to make the Lutheran Church of America more fully inclusive.

Riffat Hassan, a direct descendant of Muhammad, explains why and how the situation of Muslim women is exceptional, shows how the Quran *has been misinterpreted in ways detrimental to women, and reports that despite governmental repression, there is indeed a Muslim women's liberation movement. Finally, Jewish scholar Ellen M. Umansky describes her invisibility as a Jew in feminist gatherings, as an American in Zionist gatherings, and as a woman within both Judaism and American society; she calls for women of faith to use our power to oppose all imagery that dehumanizes any group of people anywhere.*

7

The Call of Women in the Church Today

Rosemary Radford Ruether

What is the special or unique calling of women in Christian churches today? There are dangers to this question. The question is often posed in terms of a concept of woman's "uniqueness" as different from and opposite to males; it is answered in terms of trying to find a different or distinct role for women in the church, a role that corresponds to the "feminine nature." Underneath this type of answer lies a model of complementary male and female "natures" and roles: men are the head, women the heart; men the actors; women the nurturers. Therefore, if women have a role and a ministry, it cannot be the same as men's. Women should be the comforters and nurturers, perhaps the hospital visitors, the catechists of children, and so forth. We all know where that ends up—in auxiliary and powerless roles.

DR. ROSEMARY RADFORD RUETHER is Georgia Harkness Professor of Applied Theology at Garrett-Evangelical Theological Seminary and Northwestern University in Evanston, Illinois. She has also taught at Howard University, Yale Divinity School, and Harvard Divinity School. The author or editor of seventeen books and hundreds of articles, she also lectures widely.

In contrast to this model of thought, I would deny that there are in the church special roles to which women are called. None of the leadership roles in the church are roles for which women are in any way disqualified by virtue of actual abilities. Neither large muscles nor male genitalia are relevant to preaching the Gospel or administering the sacraments. Women have always been as capable as men for all of the leadership roles in the church.

It is interesting that the original vision of the Christian community in the New Testament is *not* modeled after the family, in which mothering and fathering are different roles. On the contrary, we enter Jesus' vision of the church by leaving our families behind us. "If anyone comes to me and is not in tension with [their] own father and mother, wife and children, brothers and sisters, [they] cannot be my disciple," are his startling words (Luke 14:26). When Jesus' mother and brothers come to get him, he rejects them and points to his disciples as being his new brothers and sisters (Matthew 12:48). In Matthew 22 it is said that we are to call no man father, master, or Lord on earth, for the greatest of us is to be as a servant, even as Christ comes not to be served but to serve (Matthew 22:4–12). The church thus sees itself as a new kind of community, outside of the natural communities of family and state, calling us to a new relationship of equality and mutual service in which the traditional roles of sex, race, and class have been overcome. As St. Paul put it, "In Christ there is neither male nor female, Jew nor Greek, slave nor free" (Galatians 3:24).

Today we need to see that all of the functions in the church without exception are equally open to all persons of both sexes. However, once we have discarded the model of complementary and "special" roles, there are very distinct and unique roles and callings for women in the church today, corresponding to the uniqueness of our historic period and women's call to be witnesses in these times. The question of women's role today is to be answered from a different perspective, namely, from a recognition of the way in which the long historic oppression of women has shaped our religion, our culture, and our social institutions (and specifically the church) on pathological, dualistic, and hierarchical patterns of domination and subordination. It is the special calling of women in the church today to be witnesses against dehumanizing patterns of relationships in the church and society, and to raise up the Gospel vision of a new humanity in a new society.

What are some of the aspects of the pathological relationships that have shaped our social relationships and that the church itself has too often justified? First of all there is the idea that male headship is the divinely ordained order of nature and society and therefore of the church as well. All social prejudices have been defended as expressions of "nature" and the order of creation. In classical antiquity Aristotle justified slavery, racism, and the subordination of women by arguing that males of the ruling class and race are the natural masters of society; women, slaves, and foreign races are their natural servants. The order of creation, according to Aristotle, is one of mastery and servitude, similar to the headship of the mind over the body.

These views unfortunately have had a pervasive effect on Christian social teachings down through the centuries. Thomas Aquinas adopted Aristotle's view that woman was a "misbegotten male," an intrinsically inferior creature, defective intellectually, physically, and in the capacity for self-control. Only the male represented "perfect" humanity; and therefore Christ was incarnated in the male form. Only the male can be an image of Christ. Aquinas drew from this the conclusion that women could not be ordained. Their defective natures were incapable of receiving the "imprint" of ordination. He also thought that slaves could not be ordained either. Ordination is for those who bear the image of headship in society, and women and slaves are servile folk.

These ideas of male headship as the order of creation obviously (at least to us) come from the projection upon nature of a certain social order (namely, patriarchy), and the assertion that the pattern of social relations found in the social order has to be the way it is because that is the "nature" of the created order. Because it is the order of creation, the pattern cannot be changed. Any change in it would subvert nature and turn the world into chaos, an argument that was still being used in the debates about the Equal Rights Amendment. Indeed, among the new conservatives — the Moral Majority or the "profamily" movement — these traditional views are on the rise again. The effects of the patriarchal pattern of male headship and female submission are not limited to the relationships of men and women in the family. It becomes an archetypal pattern in patriarchal culture and religion, shaping all relations. God is seen as the top of the hierarchical system. He is envisioned as a ruling-class male, a patriarch. Creation or creatureliness is seen as a female principle utterly dependent on its Lord.

Similarly, the relationship of Yahweh and Israel in the Hebrew Scriptures, and Christ and the church in the New Testament, are modeled on the patriarchal marriage relationship. Whereas in the Hebrew Scriptures this concept of the marital relationship between God and Israel probably made the divine-human relationship seem more intimate, in the New Testament, especially Ephesians 5:22–24, it has the opposite effect. The Lordship of Christ over the church is compared to the relationship of head and body, and then this is hierarchically interpreted as being the model for marriage. The wife is told to submit to her husband as to the Lord Christ — a concept that smacks of idolatry.

Needless to say, the patriarchal marriage image of Christ and the church was soon used as an image of the relationship of the clergy over the laity, although this does not actually occur in the New Testament. This image has recently been used by both Roman Catholics and conservative Episcopalians to argue that women cannot be ordained, since they cannot be husbands. One Anglican even argued that for women to be ordained would be cosmic lesbianism. This argument stems from the idea that the priest, symbolizing Christ, has entered into a marriage relationship with the church, his bride. One wonders whether this is also supposed to mean that there should be only women in the laity; otherwise the priest would be entering into a homosexual relationship with lay males. But such arguments have never suffered from consistency!

In Christendom — that is to say, in the period between the fourth and nineteenth centuries when the church enjoyed an established relationship with the state — the patriarchal marriage relationship was also used as a political image for the relationship of the Christian sovereign to his subjects. The patriarchal model of the state was used in the early modern period to reject democracy and to declare democratic concepts of government to be contrary to God's will.

The patriarchal image was also applied to the internal relations of the self. The soul or reason is seen as masculine, the body and the passions as feminine. Hence, the body and the passions are viewed as weak, vacillating, and tending toward evil, properly to be controlled and mastered by the mind. This concept of the mind as masculine and feelings as feminine continues to be endorsed by today's psychologists as it was, in somewhat different ways, by both Freud and Jung. All of these images interlock to make the relationship of male domination and female subordination appear to be the only good, natural, and proper one.

Some people today are willing to recognize the injustice of this model of male-female relations. Women have gradually emancipated themselves from patriarchal laws and have won rights to property ownership, higher education, civil rights, and professional employment, rights that had been denied them over the millennia by patriarchal law codes. Women's actual performance in education and jobs has proven that the myths of women's inferior intellect and ability were false.

Even the 1956 Vatican declaration against women's ordination is willing to concede that women and men should be equal in secular society and that the Gospel teaches this! But the Vatican still teaches that there is some intrinsic maleness about God and Christ in the religious order that mandates the maleness of the priest. What we see here is an interesting new dilemma for the church. The symbolic patriarchy of the divine or supernatural order has lost its underpinnings in the patriarchal order of society and seeks to be its own justification. It is important to see that this patriarchal symbolism of God and Christ is based on a projection of the social order. Once that social order is pulled out from under it, the whole hierarchical superstructure in religion falls to the ground. It is not logical to claim (as the Vatican declaration tries to do) that the Gospel teaches equality in a secular society and then sanctifies some supernatural patriarchy in the religious realm.

I am inclined to think that the suppression of women and the fear and rejection of the body and sexuality took on yet another meaning in Christian asceticism, which became the norm for celibate priesthood in the late patristic period. The escape from sexuality and reproduction was seen as an escape from mortality. Carnality, mutability, and mortality are the signs of our finitude, tying us to the cycle of birth and death. To extract the divine spark of the soul from the body with its needs for food, sex, and sleep, is somehow to elevate oneself to the higher realms of the eternal and everlasting, secure against the threat of death. The fear of sex was ultimately an expression of the fear of death.

This ascetic tradition has left us a fearful legacy of pathological attitudes toward sexuality. Sexuality is linked to sin and hence to death. Those who would be pure must be as asexual as possible. This heritage has given Western culture, even in its secular form, a repressive-exploitative view of sex and hence of sexual relations with women. Even libertine and pornographic indulgence in sex is finally just the other side of the coin of the fearful and repressive view. Sex is dirty, and thus one can either shun it or roll in it, in increasingly sadistic and violent ways. But never does one arrive at a healthy balance where the body and sex are used as expressions of joy and mutuality. Pornography and asceticism are two sides of the same diseased view of the self from which our culture still suffers.

We might include here the pathology of homophobia as one of the legacies of patriarchal sexism. Patriarchy sees sexual relations as those of subject and object, of mastery and subjugation. Therefore, for a man to have relations with another man is a degrading abomination because it treats another man like a woman (Leviticus 18:22). It is said that sex must be the union of opposites, the union of maleness and femaleness, action and passivity. Therefore, homosexual relations are incomplete and narcissistic. Finally, sexual union must be procreative, for procreation is the only purpose of sex, and homosexual relations cannot be procreative. It is interesting to see Protestant thinkers adopt this argument against homosexuals even though they have abandoned the procreative view of sexual relations between men and women. Therefore, homosexuality is an abomination, contrary to the natural order.

All of this skirts the possibility that sex might be an expression of love, an expression not of subject and object, or of two halves of a polarized humanity, but rather a union of subject and subject, of two whole and full human beings responding to one another as persons. Male-female attrac-

tion might be the orientation of 90 percent of the population, but since human sexuality is interpersonal and not just
biological, there is no reason that a minority might not be
different. The recent Catholic Theological Society's study on
human sexuality has suggested that homosexuality be looked
at as a normal human deviation, somewhat like left-handed-
ness. The same standards of loving mutuality by which we
define heterosexual sexuality as moral, should be applied to
homosexuals as well.

Having looked at some of the pathologies of patriarchal
and ascetic religion, let us ask about women's liberation as a
witness to a new humanity. Once patriarchal pathologies
become clear, the unique role of women emerging from patriarchal suppression also becomes clear. The special calling
of women in the church today is to be a witness to a new
humanity and to call the church and its religious symbols
back to their original meaning as harbingers of a redeemed
and reconciled human order. Wherever the liberation of
women threatens the old understanding of social relations,
there is an opportunity to open up again the true meaning of
redemption, and to envision possibilities for a fulfilled existence that has been denied us.

On many different levels we can see the liberating sign of
the new woman in the church. The first important effect of
the revolt against patriarchy is the emancipation of the doctrine of nature from its misuse as a rationalization for
hierarchical social systems. This begins with the liberal affirmation that God created all persons equally and endowed
them with the same basic human natures, from which flow
the same civil rights and liberties. This concept of nature, of
course, underlies the revolutionary principles of the French
and American revolutions. It was first enunciated to over-
throw the old feudal and aristocratic order of Christendom.
Unfortunately, the Catholic church had linked itself with
this feudal, aristocratic order, and so, for two centuries,

made itself the enemy of the liberal doctrines of equality and freedom.

Many Christian thinkers, such as the abolitionist-feminist Sarah Grimke, quickly recognized in the liberal doctrine of nature the vindication of the true Gospel vision. God did not create the world as a hierarchy of master and slave, but created all persons, male and female, equally in the divine image. Mastery and servitude are expressions of sin, not expressions of God's will for the natural order. Redemption, therefore, means a social struggle to emancipate blacks and women from relations of servitude, and to restore equal personhood in the divine image as the true "order of creation." This interpretation of redemption, formulated in the early nineteenth century, was the foundation of the Social Gospel movement, and, later, of the theology of liberation. Salvation is not an other-worldly flight from creation to heaven purchased by enduring unjust relations on earth, but rather it is the struggle to create the new heaven and earth where, as Jesus said, "God's will is done on earth, as it is in heaven." This understanding of redemption reclaims its roots in Jewish messianic hope.

The emancipation of women is a prophetic sign in many other ways as well. It is a sign of a many-sided struggle to overcome the pathological relationships of sexist culture. It is a sign of the struggle to create new models of relationships between men and women in the family and in society. Men and women should understand their partnership in the family not as one of mastery or servitude, or even of complementary opposites. Rather the family partnership is a covenant of mutuality in which each pledges to work for the full human realization of the other. A woman who remains confined to the home, with rote domestic labor and without an opportunity to use her intelligence in the larger world, is being deprived of her full humanity. Likewise, a man who is in a rat race of economic advancement that gives him less and less time for the cultivation of his mind, emotions, and cultural sensitivities, and that cuts him off from his children, is being deprived of full humanity. We need a new covenant of mutuality for the family that apportions the roles so that both men and women have a balance of work and leisure, equal opportunities for action in society, and nurturance of the self and others in their families. This, and not the shrill anti-ERA, antifeminist diatribes of the so-called "profamily movement," is the real key to renewal of the family.

Such a renewal of the family also demands a vast reordering of society as well, giving women equal opportunities on the job. The very nature of work needs to be examined. Principles such as shared decisions and worker self-management of workplaces give us an idea of what a more humanized economic order might look like.

The whole area of sexual repression and exploitation is another matter that must be addressed by women. Churchmen fear women in equal roles with them largely because the church is rooted in their suppressed and insecure sexuality. Such men can scarcely imagine working with women as colleagues. To be alone together is to open the gates to seduction or rape. Only by rigid repression and segregation of the sexes is it possible to maintain control. However, those men who revolt against sexual repression may identify sexual liberation with dehumanized promiscuity. Increasingly our rejection of the old repression leads to a pornographic culture of sexual violence and sadism. Only a sexuality rooted in friendship, rooted in mutual respect and love, can redeem us from this fearful dichotomy of puritanism and pornography. The first step to this is the emergence of women who insist on being respected rather than being reduced to sexual objects. We need to see that pornography is not a liberal civil right: it is the propagation of exploitation and violence toward women, and should be treated in our society with no more sympathy than we would treat the advocacy of lynching and castration of blacks.

It is often asked what the church and religion have to do with all this. If patriarchal religion has been the deepest source of the legitimization of sexism, and is still today its chief mainstay, why not abandon it and get on with the liberation of women in society? There is nothing wrong with getting on with the business of liberation of women in society. Yet the churches and synagogues are not to be ignored. Certainly some of us should find our vocation in dealing with them in particular. There are several reasons for this. First of all, religion provides the oldest and most authoritative legitimization of sexism in society. So the transformation of that authority, by putting religion on the side of liberation, is not insignificant. Religion, more than any other institution, provides the symbols of ultimate meaning. Thus to show those symbols as liberating will have far deeper transformative effects than can take place on just the secular level alone.

Thus, a struggle to liberate the social institutions of the religious communities is particularly important. If the Gospel stands for the liberation of persons, then the church itself should be the first paradigm of the liberated community rather than the last bastion of sexism. The particular calling of women in the church, therefore, is to help the church become a more authentic symbol. This entails not only the opening up of all ministries (ordained and unordained) to women. It also involves a transformation of the very nature of ministry, so that ministry becomes empowerment of others toward the creation of a community of mutual service, rather than the reduction of the laity to sheep led by the shepherd. One of the important signs of the depth of the present women's ordination movement in the Catholic church is that it has clearly grasped this double agenda: not only to include women in the ordained ministry, but to transform ministry itself into the New Testament model of mutual service, rather than the power of some over others.

Finally, the witness of women in the church must transform our traditional language about God. Too long has God been used as a symbol of the top of the hierarchy of social oppression. This is nothing less than idolatry and blasphemy, for it makes of God a sanction for evil. God is not the biggest white male king in the system. God is the transcendent center of liberated personhood in the community; God is Creator, Redeemer, and Sustainer of our authentic life. In the New Testament understanding of Christ, God has abdicated the role of upholding and sanctifying the system of domination and is emptied out to become the servant and liberator of creation. When we stop manipulating God as exclusively He or She, when we stop using God as an object in our power games and encounter the living God, who is not He, She, or It, but *Thou*, then we will discover the power to give up our security-and-domination games and empty ourselves out in service to each other to create the new heaven and new earth.

Women have a calling in the churches today: a calling to represent that liberating sign of new humanity, precisely because they have so long endured so much oppression and deprivation of full humanity. We might reflect on the fact that the New Testament puts into the mouth of Mary (the representative of the messianic Israel) one of the most dramatic statements of revolution that has ever been written:

> The One who is Mighty has done great things for me . . .
> [God] has scattered the proud in the imagination of their hearts,
> put down the mighty from their thrones, and exalted those of low degree,
> filled the hungry with good things, and sent the rich empty away.

8

The Struggle of a Black Lutheran

Mary L. Chrichlow

I know well the struggle for identity, for my life began as a struggle. According to sociologists, neither my two brothers nor I would be able to make it because we had inherent in us the pathology for failure that was the inheritance of many black people born in this country during the 1920s. Like our parents and grandparents, we were black (called colored or Negro then). We were born in the South about the time of the Great Depression; we were raised by our mother alone; we were disadvantaged and underprivileged and should have remained that way. We should have perpetuated that pathology. But we had a mother who passed on to us something more precious than silver and gold and worldly posses-

MARY L. CHRICHLOW formerly directed the National Conference of Christians and Jews in the Long Island, New York area; she is currently a consultant in human relations and interfaith relations. A member of New Hope Lutheran Church in Jamaica, Long Island, she chairs the synod transition team for the metropolitan New York area. For the Lutheran Church of America, she serves on the management committee of the Division for Professional Leadership, and on the board of the Lutheran seminaries in Philadelphia and Columbia, South Carolina. She is a member of the Parkhurst Civic Association, and of the board of directors of Franklin General Hospital and the Queens Federation of Churches. She and her husband are the grandparents of three.

sions or opinions—something that was hers which she prayed we would grasp, something that could never be taken away from us if we would only remember it.

First, Mama strongly believed and had faith in God as the controller of all things. To her, everything began and ended with God. Therefore, she made and kept peace with God.

Second, she trusted the will of the Lord and surrendered to Him.

Third, she gave thanks and praise to the Lord for all things—even for us when we did not live up to her wishes.

Fourth, our Mother had dignity. She was respectful of herself and gave respect to all whom she met. She demanded dignity in others' treatment of her and would become angry if she felt that she was not getting it. But she was also humble. We never heard her boast about anything concerning herself or us.

Finally and most of all, Mama *loved*: her God, her family, all people. She did not waste energy hating those who hated her. She treated them kindly and turned them over to the Lord because she believed that justice was in His hands. She took literally scriptural teaching: faith is the substance of things hoped for, the evidence of things unseen.

It is that faith, undergirded with prayer, which has sustained me throughout my life in the most difficult, hurtful situations. It has sustained me in the Lutheran church. I was not born a Lutheran. I converted to Lutheranism when, with my husband and young son, I moved into a white community and the pastor of the local Lutheran church went out of his way to welcome us. This was appreciated especially because members of the congregation were resistant to us and the white neighbors began to run from the area as blacks moved in. It hurt to see religious people, Christians and Jews, flee from us because, to them, we were members of a group to be feared.

Lutheranism has been an awakening experience, both spiritually and culturally. Over these thirty-odd years, I have worked endlessly in efforts to make the Lutheran Church in America (LCA) an inclusive church that accepts all members as full participants — not only in local congregations, but in decision-making bodies throughout the organization. It has not been easy. Although the LCA has issued a number of social statements and resolutions dealing with racism, minority concerns, and issues of justice, it is struggling against a background of conservatism, exclusiveness, and rigidity.

A key social statement, "Race Relations," was adopted by the LCA at its convention in 1964, and some strides have been made toward eliminating racism from the church in subsequent conventions. In 1978, the LCA convention adopted a social statement on "Goals and Plans for Minority Ministry" that proposed a five-year plan by which the church would continue to be more inclusive in membership while expanding its emphasis on justice in society. But, as we know, the wheels of justice grind slowly without lubrication. Thus, in 1977, it was necessary for blacks to organize the Association of Black Lutherans, designed to be a vehicle for unification and to express the needs and concerns of black members of the LCA through existing LCA structures. The group has seven purposes and has made significant progress and achievements. The purposes are:

1. to encourage maximum participation of black persons in the ongoing program of the church, and in the conception, design, and implementation of new programs;
2. to raise the consciousness of blacks regarding their cultural and social heritage, emphasizing those factors that have been strengths for the black community throughout the years;
3. to assist LCA synods, agencies, institutions, and congregations in better understanding black culture and incorpo-

rating from that culture those practices which will enhance the church and make it more reflective of its
membership;

4. to assist the LCA in implementing "Goals and Plans for
Minority Ministry";
5. to actively recruit and support black youths and adults for
church vocations;
6. to advocate unrestricted mobility for black leadership
(clergy and laity), opening up positions in institutions,
congregations, synods, and church-wide agencies;
7. to focus theological education to include urban concerns
and black culture.

While the association is racially oriented, it is not racist.
Membership is open to all active members of LCA congrega-
tions who subscribe to the goals and objectives set forth.
Incidentally, the president of the association is a woman.

Since history is important to a people, particularly if they
are going to experience participatory democracy, a committee was formed in 1978 to trace the history of blacks in the
Lutheran church and to give them a sense of belonging by
"telling the story" of what it has meant to be black and
Lutheran (from the time of the first black Lutheran) and
what it means today, and to point realistically toward the
future. Just as Alex Haley stimulated pride in heritage by
tracing his roots, black Lutherans were encouraged to learn
that they were not latecomers in the church. We have a
history in the Lutheran church from its very beginning in
this country in the 1600s; black ordinations date back as
early as the 1800s. Although research has been difficult due
to inadequate record keeping, a paper titled "Black and Lutheran" has been published, and others are anticipated.

The church has come a long way, but there is still a long
way to go before the affirmative, accepting spirit embraces
all of its members. In 1988, three Lutheran church bodies
will merge and already committees are working together to

ensure that the progress made in opening up the churches is coordinated and advanced.

Effecting change is a slow, painful, frustrating process that demands total involvement of time, talent, and often treasury. Not many minority people can give such total commitment; the few who can become overworked. I overextend myself because I know that even one person can make a difference. Many times, I am the only woman on a board or committee. I work on committees in my local congregation. For the national Church, I serve on two seminary boards, one in the northeast and one in the southeast, as well as on a management committee board. I serve on the board of the Lutheran Human Relations Association in America, and am active in the Association of Black Lutherans. I worked on the "Black and Lutheran" project.

I am concerned particularly about Lutheran interreligious relations and am involved in Lutheran-Catholic and Lutheran-Jewish dialogues, as well as the design task force on interfaith and ecumenical relations for the New Lutheran Church. During 1984, which marked the observance of the five hundreth birthday of Martin Luther, Lutherans were sharply reminded that some of Luther's attitudes and writings are perceived as anti-Catholic and anti-Jewish (some feel they are anti-Semitic). As a woman who has been sensitized through suffering, I wonder how Luther would have received blacks. I am grateful that my faith has given me the stamina to look past old hurts and slights and has made me more determined to work to make the Lutheran church what it professes to be: a church of people who love all people, as commanded by God.

I am not merely a Sunday Christian. My religious concern carries over into my daily living: with my family, friends, and work, and in community organizations and activities. I chose to work for the National Conference of Christians and Jews for many years because its goals were so in tune with my personal belief: we are all brothers and sisters under one God and should realize our interdependency. We must be concerned about dignity and the equality of justice for all people regardless of religion, race, color, creed, national origin, sex, age, or class.

This brings me to what I see as a challenge for women of faith. Is there a special role or need for us? As we look around and really see (mentally and spiritually with our inner eye and heart), we become sensitive to injustices in society; we become conscious of the sick, hungry, the imprisoned, the lonely, the disabled and disadvantaged, those who suffer crippling afflictions and addictions. We know that change is needed. Since men have been running the world from time immemorial and problems continue mounting, we see the challenge falling to us. We should grasp the opportunity to affect the whole of our social and human fabric.

In her book *Women of the Bible*, Edith Deans tells of all the changes brought about by women of biblical times; one of my favorites is Esther. We know of many such women in our own time. Traditionally, we have had to assume — and must continue to assume — the obligation to redevelop and re-create a renewed feeling of love and joy of life, a zest for living, a new pride in being human, a new hope that there is something to look forward to — in brief, a rebirth of the perennial religious and philosophical concept that we are all one family under one God. And this means, of course, that we must work together to be able to defeat and destroy the real bane of our society: the apathy, sense of detachment, disinterest in the fate of our neighbor, and unconcern with one another that surrounds us all.

A word about power. We are in a power-oriented age and society, but we often forget the strongest power, prayer: we put it last. It might take a long time to come to the realization, but most of us, after trying all roads and methods, finally resort to prayer. Some time ago, I was in an audience of "women achievers" listening to prominent, successful women tell how they made it. One said, "I worked hard, took advantage of every opportunity — and I prayed." Then she added,

> Let me caution you about prayer — it works. Therefore, you must be careful; your prayers may be answered and you might discover that what you get is not what you wanted. Now, I pray "open-ended." I leave the rest up to God who has the power.

Personally, I take it a step farther: I pray as if all depends on God and work as if all depends on me!

In the beginning of my presentation, I spoke of my mother who gave me a legacy of abiding faith, hope, and love. I would like to close with the words of another black woman, educator and humanitarian Mary McLeod Bethune, who has had a great influence upon my life. In her "Last Will and Testament" she wrote:

> I leave you a thirst for education. Knowledge is the prime need of the hour. I leave you a respect for the uses of power. I leave you faith. Faith is the first factor in a life devoted to service. Without faith, nothing is possible. I leave you racial dignity. Maintain your dignity at all costs. I leave you responsible to our young people. I leave you love; love builds. It is positive and helpful. I leave you hope. I leave you a desire to live harmoniously with your fellow man [and woman]. I pray that my philosophy may be helpful to those who share my vision for a world of Peace, Progress, [Sisterhood,] Brotherhood, and Love.

9

Women in the Context of Change and Confrontation within Muslim Communities

Riffat Hassan

Islam has been a living reality for over fourteen hundred years, but it took the Arab oil embargo of 1973 and the Iranian Revolution of 1979 to awaken many people from their "dogmatic slumber" to take note of the fact that Islam was not quite dead after all. In the wake of the so-called "revival" of what had been presumed to be a dead or dying Islam, many questions have been asked about the fundamental nature, value system, and historical development of the Islamic way of life. Since we have lived in the midst of a feminist revolution in the West, it is not surprising that questions related to the position of Muslim women figure promi-

DR. RIFFAT HASSAN chairs the religious studies program at the University of Louisville. A native of Pakistan and a direct descendant of Muhammad, she has published many articles and two books on Iqbal Muhammad. Currently she is writing a book titled *Equal before Allah? A Feminist Study of Issues Pertaining to Woman-Man Equality, Discussed in the Light of the Qur'an, with Observations on Women-Related Ideas and Attitudes in the Judaeo-Christian-Islamic Traditions.*

nently among the questions asked about Islam. Two other factors responsible for focusing attention on Muslim women have been the role of the Iranian women in their revolution and the execution of a Saudi Arabian princess. Each of these factors illustrate, in profound ways, the phenomena of change and confrontation as they relate to women in many Muslim communities today.

Since the "modern" period of Islamic history began with the colonization of most Muslim countries, many changes have occurred in these countries. Some of these changes have visibly affected the lives of women. In a number of Muslim countries, there is a marked improvement in the situation as far as women's education and employment are concerned. Also in many Muslim countries women have acquired important legal and political rights. So it would seem to be the case—from one point of view—that Muslim women are coming out of the Dark Ages and that it is only a matter of time before they will take their rightful place in human society and cease to be the largest (more than four hundred million) and perhaps the most oppressed minority in the world. Although the statistics relating to the improving situation of women (particularly in the areas of education and employment) are signs of hope, in my opinion they cannot be said to reflect the whole truth regarding the lot of women in Muslim societies.

Despite the fact that there are many parallels among the ways in which the Jewish, Christian, and Islamic traditions have regarded women, there are some ways in which the situation of Muslim women is exceptional. Through their long and arduous struggle against sexism, many Jewish and Christian women acquired the ability to describe their search for self-identity and the meaning of their existence. For the majority of Muslim women who have been kept for centuries in physical, mental, and emotional bondage and deprived of opportunities to see themselves as fully human, the task of defining what womanhood in Islam is, or even of analyzing their personal experiences as Muslim women, is quite overwhelming.

Even when a Muslim woman is able to acquire an education and secure a job, she is seldom able to free herself from the burden of traditionalism that confronts her on all sides. In the absence of any supportive literature or any social support structure, it is very difficult for the small majority of self-aware Muslim women to deal with the kind of oppression that prevails in Muslim societies. So, although there are changes taking place in Muslim societies due to a variety of socio-economic, historic, or political factors, in few Muslim countries is one likely to encounter such a dramatic confrontation as the one between the "chador-clad" women and the "jeans-clad" women of postrevolutionary Iran.

But the fact that confrontations are rare does not mean that there is no conflict in Muslim societies between men and women or between the traditional and the modern. In my judgment what we are witnessing today is the beginning of one of Islam's greatest revolutions, the women's revolution, even though many Muslims insist that the women's struggle — for example, in Iran — is nothing but a political stunt or a divisive tactic employed by leftists to tarnish the radiance of Iran's glorious revolution. It is easy enough to mock at the magnitude of the Iranian women's struggle by reducing it to a Lilliput-style feud between women who wear the chador and women who wear jeans. But behind the cartoons and the slogans is a terrifying reality that threatens to shake the world of Islam from within. Reluctance or refusal to face this reality is liable to lead to very serious consequences. Forces of Islamic conservatism are straining hard to keep the lid of Pandora's box from flying off, but it is the verdict of history that a genuine revolution, once begun, will run its course.

All thinking Muslims know that the world of Islam is

faced with a very severe crisis. Some realize that a major reason for this crisis is the fact that though so many people are suddenly talking about Islam, most people, including most Muslims, do not know except vaguely what they mean by Islam. If one asks an "average" Muslim what he understands by Islam, he is likely to refer to one or more of the following: the Quran (the Book of Revelation), the *Sunnah* and *Hadith* (the practice and sayings ascribed to the Prophet of Islam), *Fiqh* (jurisprudence), *Madahib* (schools of law), and the *Shari'ah* (the code of laws regulating all aspects of Muslim life). If all the above mentioned "sources" of Islam formed a coherent, homogeneous body of knowledge, perhaps one could include all of them in the term Islam. But not only are there numerous problems of inner inconsistency within the area of *Hadith* and *Sunnah* and the schools of law; it also does not seem possible in my opinion to resolve the conflicts between the different "sources" of Islam.

Because there is no consensus among Muslims as to what Islam is, it becomes virtually impossible to talk about the Islamic view of women or the normative view of women according to Islam's theoretical perspective without first defining what one means by Islam.

In terms of my own research, which I hope will soon be published, I define Islam strictly in terms of what is contained in the Quran. I do so because the centrality of the Quran to the Islamic world view and belief system is undisputed. Also, in view of the Muslim belief that the Quran is the Word of Allah conveyed through the agency of the Angel Gabriel to the Prophet Muhammad and transmitted by him without any error or changes to those who heard him, the degree of authority possessed by the Quran is "absolute," whereas the authority of the other sources of Islam is "relative"—at least theoretically. The majority of the Muslims in the world, however, though they acknowledge the Quran to be the basic document on which Islam is founded, are influ-

enced much more by what is contained in the *Hadith* literature and the *Shari'ah* than they are by the Quran. This is not
surprising since the Quran is generally understood in the
light of commentaries (*tafsirs*), which are themselves based
upon *Hadith* literature or the explanations of the jurists (*fu-
qaha*), whose main source of information is also the *Hadith*
literature.

Keeping in mind, then, that a state of confusion generally prevails in the Muslim mind with regard to Islamic
ideals, let us focus on five areas of special concern to Muslim
women.

The first area to draw our attention is the attitude to
female children. The Quran forbade the practice of female
infanticide in a number of verses (for example sura 81, verses
8 and 9; sura 16, verses 57–59; sura 17, verse 31). Muslims
today do not bury their daughters alive as they did not infre-
quently in pre-Islamic Arabia. In most Muslim societies,
however, there is jubilation when a son is born and sadness
or at best silence when a daughter is born. Most Muslims do
not think that the Quranic condemnation of the killing of
daughters also includes the ethical principle that daughters
are not to be discriminated against in favor of sons. If a
Muslim woman produces only daughters, she is likely to be
subjected to humiliation and persecution and threatened
with divorce. As women become more literate and self-
aware in Muslim societies they become acutely resentful of
being discriminated against from the moment of birth.
There is urgent need in Muslim societies, therefore, for an
enlightened attitude toward female children.

The second area of interest is male-female relationships,
especially in the context of marriage. The Quran makes it
clear that God made man and woman in like manner, of like
substance (for example, sura 4, verse 1; sura 7, verse 189;
sura 16, verse 72; sura 42, verse 11) and that man and woman are, in every way, equal in the sight of God (sura 3, verse

195; sura 16, verse 97; sura 4, verse 124; sura 9, verses 71–72; sura 4, verse 32). Nonetheless, Muslim societies have sought to subvert the intent of these passages by citing traditions that describe Eve (whose name is not mentioned in the Quran) as created from the crooked rib of Adam[1] and as being responsible for Adam's fall from grace. (There is no suggestion in the Quran that Eve was a secondary creation made from Adam's rib, nor that she was a temptress who through her evil, vanity, foolishness, and weakness caused Adam's fall).

It is taken as a self-evident truth in all Muslim societies that men, in general, are superior to women, and that the husband in particular is superior to the wife. I have spent much time investigating the religious sources of this idea and have come to the conclusion that it is based primarily on some Quranic verses and a number of traditions ascribed to the Prophet. The critical examination of this material is of crucial importance: without it no fundamental change in the position of woman can occur in any Muslim society.

Sura 4, verse 34, is perhaps the most important Quranic verse dealing with the subject of men and women. Before I share with you my own understanding of this verse — and I have "wrestled" with this verse for years — let me quote Abdullah Yusuf 'Ali's translation of it:

> Men are the protectors
> And maintainers of women,
> Because God has given
> The one more [strength]
> Than the other, and because
> they support them from their means.
> Therefore the righteous women
> Are devoutly obedient, and guard
> In [the husband's] absence
> What God would have them guard.
> As to those women

On whose part ye fear
Disloyalty and ill-conduct,
Admonish them [first]
[Next], refuse to share their beds,
[And last] beat them lightly
But if they return to obedience,
Seek not against them
Means [of annoyance]
For God is Most-High
Great [above you all][2]

It is assumed by almost all who read this verse that it is addressed to husbands. The first point to be noted is that it is addressed to *ar-rijal* ("the men") and to *an- nisaa* ("the women"). In other words, it is addressed to all men and women of the Islamic community. This is further indicated by the fact that in relation to all the actions that are required to be taken, the plural and not the dual form (used when reference is made to two persons) is found. Such usage makes clear that the orders contained in this verse were not addressed to a husband or wife but to the Islamic *ummah* (community) in general.

The key word in the first sentence of this verse is *qawwamun*. This word has been translated variously as "protectors and maintainers [of women]," "in charge [of women]," "having pre-eminence [above women]," and "sovereigns or masters [over women]." Linguistically, the word *qawwamun* means "breadwinners" or "those who provide a means of living." A point of logic that must be made here is that the first sentence is not a descriptive one stating that all men *as a matter of fact* are providing for women, since obviously there are at least some men who do not provide for women. What the sentence is stating, rather, is that men ought to have the capability to provide (since *ought* implies *can*). In other words this statement, which almost all Muslim societies have taken to be an actual description of all men, is in fact a normative statement pertaining to the Islamic concept of division of labor in an ideal family structure. The fact that men are *qawwamun* does not mean that women cannot or should not provide for themselves, but simply that in view of the heavy burden that most women shoulder with regard to family duties, they should not have the additional *obligation* of providing the means of living.

Continuing with the analysis of sura 4, verse 34, we come next to the idea that God has given *the one* more strength than the other. Most translations make it appear that the one who has more strength, excellence, or superiority is the man. However, the Quranic expression does not accord superiority to man. The expression literally means "some in relation to some," so that the statement could mean either that some men are superior to some others (men and/or women) and that some women are superior to some others (men and/or women). In my opinion, what is being stated here is that some men are more blessed with the means to be better providers than are other men.

The next part of the verse begins with a "therefore," which indicates that this part is conditional upon the first: in other words, if men fulfill their assigned function of being providers, women must fulfill their corresponding duties. Most translations describe this duty in terms of the wife being "obedient" to the husband. The word *salihat*, which is translated as "righteously obedient," is related to the word *salahiat*, which means "capability" or "potentiality," and not obedience. Women's special capability is to bear children. The word *qanitat* which succeeds the word *salihat* and is also translated as "obedient" is related to a water bag in which water is carried from one place to another without spilling. The woman's special function, then, according to this verse, is that like the bag in which water is transported without loss to its destination, she carries and protects the fetus in her womb until it can be safely delivered.

What is outlined in the first part of this verse is a functional division of labor necessary for maintaining balance in any society. Men who do not have to fulfill the responsibility of childbearing are assigned the function of being breadwinners. Women are exempted from the responsibility of being breadwinners in order that they may fulfill their function as childbearers. The two functions are separate but complementary and neither is higher or lower than the other.

The three injunctions in the second part of the verse were given to the Islamic *ummah* in order to meet a rather extraordinary possibility: a mass rebellion on the part of women against their role as childbearers, the function assigned to them by God. If all or most of the women in a Muslim society refused to bear children without just cause as a sign of organized defiance or revolt, this would mean the end of the Muslim *ummah*. This situation must, therefore, be dealt with decisively. The first step to be taken is to counsel the rebels. If this step is unsuccessful, the second step to be taken is isolation of the rebellious women from significant others. (It is to be noted here that the prescription is "to leave the women alone in their beds." By translating this line, "refuse to share their beds," Yusef Ali is suggesting, if not stating, that the judging party is the husband and not the Islamic community — an assumption not warranted by the text.)

If the second step is also not successful, then the step of confining the women for a longer period of time may be taken by the Islamic *ummah* or its representatives. Here, it is important to point out that the Arabic word that is generally translated as "beating," when used in a legal context as it is here, means "holding in confinement," according to the authoritative lexicon *Taj al-'Arus*. (In sura 4, verse 15, unchaste women are also prescribed the punishment of being confined to their homes.)

I have analyzed sura 4, verse 34, in detail in order to show how the words of the Quran have been mistranslated in order to make men the masters and women the slaves. Most traditions dealing with the subject of married women also describe a virtuous woman as one who pleases and obeys her husband at all times. Pleasing the husband can, in fact, become more important than pleasing God since, as one tradition puts it, "the woman who does not discharge her duties to her husband is disobedient to Allah, and the discharge of duties towards Allah depends on the discharge of duties towards the husband" (Ibn Majah).[3]

A daughter is not equal to a son in Muslim societies where, in contradiction to an explicit Quranic injunction, frequently daughters (and sometimes sons) are married without their consent. This pattern of injustice reaches its climax in the husband-wife relationship in which the husband becomes the wife's gateway to heaven or hell. The fact that there is more Quranic legislation on the subject of a right ordering of the relationship between men and women than on any other subject shows how important this subject is within the framework of the Quran. That so much of this legislation has been ignored or supplanted shows how afraid Muslim societies have been of changing the existing balance of power in the domain of family relationships.

The third topic for our attention is polygamy. Islam has been much attacked for its support of polygamy, but polygamy is allowed by the Quran only in very exceptional circumstances and with a very rigid requirement attached to it. Sura 2, verses 2 and 3, which contain the only reference to polygamy in the Quran, reads as follows:

> To orphans restore their property —
> [When they reach their age],
> Nor substitute [your] worthless things
> For [their] good ones; and devour not
> Their substance [by mixing it up]
> With your own. For this is

Indeed a great sin.
But if ye fear that ye shall not
Be able to deal justly
With the orphans,
Marry women of your choice,
Two, or three, or four;
But if ye fear that ye shall not
be able to deal justly [with them];
The only one, or [a captive]
That your right hands possess
That will be more suitable,
To protect you
From doing injustice.[4]

Polygamy is not recommended but permitted only in special circumstances and for humanitarian purposes. The requirement to be just to all one's wives is also an absolute one. Despite these qualifications, however, it is indisputable that polygamy has been widely misused through the ages and has done tremendous damage to women.

In the last decades several "progressive" Muslim countries tried to control the practice of polygamy and divorce by reforming family law. This was a change that would have been of much benefit to women, but with the swinging of the pendulum in the direction of conservatism, the reforms are being abrogated (for example, in Iran). There is some weakening in the institution of polygamy due to economic factors, and with more monogamous marriages the incidence of divorce is also likely to decrease.

Our fourth issue is family planning. Since in sura 17, verse 31, the Almighty promised sustenance for all offspring, family planning programs have had little success even in the poorest of Muslim countries. Another Quranic passage that is cited by opponents of birth control in Muslim societies is sura 2, verse 223, which reads:

> Your wives are
> As a tilth into you
> So approach your tilth
> When or how you will . . .[5]

Numerous traditions attributed to the Prophet insist that a wife must never refuse to have sexual relations with her husband; so meeting her husband's sexual demands becomes a woman's religious duty.

Conservative Muslims have taken a strong line against birth control. A. A. Maududi's observations are quite typical of their viewpoint:

> Coeducation, employment of women in offices, mixed social gatherings, immodest female dresses, and beauty parades are now a common feature of our social life. Legal hindrances have also been placed in the way of marriage and on having more than one wife, but no bar against keeping mistresses and illicit relationships, prior to the age of marriage. In such a society perhaps the last obstacle that may keep a woman from surrendering to a man's advances is fear of an illegitimate conception. Remove this obstacle too and provide to women with weak character assurance that they can safely surrender to their male friends and you will see that the society will be plagued by the tide of moral licentiousness.[6]

In this day and age there can be no doubt that a woman who has no control over her own body or who is compelled by social and religious pressures to play the part of a reproductive machine becomes less than a fully autonomous human being. There is a definite correlation between the social status of women and their ability to control or determine how many children they will have, as indicated by numerous studies. *Status of Women and Family Planning*, published by the United Nations (New York, 1975) is one such study. There is little doubt that the future of Muslim women depends critically on the choices open to them in the area of family planning.

Fifth, and finally, is the question of purdah. In the context of proper attire and conduct, the Quran lays down one basic principle. This may be described as the principle of modesty. In sura 24, verses 30 and 31, modesty in enjoined both upon Muslim men and Muslim women, though more detailed instructions are given in the case of women because at the dawn of Islam women were regarded as sex objects to be used as toys and bait, to be bought and sold, to be ogled and discarded at will. By using an elaborate network of laws and recommendations the Quran aimed at liberating women from the indignity of being sex objects and transforming them into *persons.* If a woman wished to be regarded as a person and not as a sex object, it was necessary, according to Quranic teaching, that she should behave with the dignity and decorum befitting a secure, self-respecting, and self-aware human being rather than as an insecure female who felt that her survival depended on her ability to attract, entertain, or cajole those men who were interested not in her personality but only in her sexuality.

Muslim societies in general have disregarded the basic intent of the Quranic statements of women's status as autonomous human beings capable of being righteous as an act of choice. These societies have preferred to regard women as mentally and morally deficient creatures on whom morality has to be externally imposed. Nothing perhaps illustrates Muslim men's deep insecurities (which are reflected in their obsession with female sexuality and the means of controlling it) so well as the sternness and strictness with which they compel their women to cover themselves from head to foot and keep them confined to their houses. (Such confinement is described by sura 4, verse 15, as a punishment for unchaste women and *not* as the normal way of life[7].)

It is beyond the scope of this paper to discuss all the areas in which a change of attitude toward women is needed, areas where conflict could be likely to erupt between those who hold opposing viewpoints. I have, however, endeavored to point out some areas of special concern to a large number of Muslim women.

With each passing day, with each new imposition, at least some Muslim women are becoming more and more aware of the burden of oppression that they have carried for so long. They are beginning to ask to exercise their rights, rights given to them not by an Islamic government but by Allah. Their struggle and its outcome cannot in the final analysis be separated from what Islam was, what it has become, and where it is going; but their struggle may very well turn the tide of events in modern history.

NOTES

1. *Sahih Muslim*, trans. A. H. Siddiqui, vol. 2, p. 753.

2. *The Holy Qur'an*, trans. Abdullah Yusuf 'Ali (Indianapolis, 1975), pp. 190–91.

3. M. Imran, *Ideal Woman in Islam* (Lahore, 1979), p. 51.

4. *The Holy Qur'an*, pp. 178–79.

5. *The Holy Qur'an*, p. 88.

6. A. A. Maududi, *Birth Control*, trans. K. Ahmad and M. I. Faruqi (Lahore, 1974), p. 176.

7. G. A. Parvez, *Tahira Kay Nam* (Lahore, 1972), p. 197.

10

Racism, Classism, and Sexism: A Jewish Woman's Perspective

Ellen M. Umansky

For as long as I can remember, I have identified myself as an American Jew. Within the last fifteen years, during the resurgence of feminism in America, I have come to identify myself more fully — as an American Jewish woman.

This identity is not without contradictions. There are times when I watch the evening news and see before me in living color those who run our government, those whose voices are heard and recorded — almost all of them men — and I feel invisible as a woman. I read articles and books, listen to scholarly lectures on American Jewish life, and recognize that it is only our fathers' world (to paraphrase the title of Irving Howe's study) that is reflected. And again, I feel invisible. I attend national feminist gatherings where

DR. ELLEN M. UMANSKY is associate professor of religion at Emory University. Affiliated with Reform Judaism, Dr. Umansky has authored two books concerning Lyly Montagu, founder and leader of the liberal Jewish movement in England. She is currently researching a book on the development of the Society of Jewish Science, a twentieth-century movement based in New York and devoted to spiritual healing within the Jewish tradition.

the unique suffering of the Jewish people is denied; where attacks against Israel thinly disguise anti-Semitic outbursts; where I am expected for the sake of sisterhood to sacrifice Jewish concerns and fears, while my non-Jewish sisters are permitted, indeed encouraged, to voice their own. And again, I feel invisible, this time as a Jew. Yet as I argue with Jewish friends over whether American Jews are in exile, whether it is only in Israel that the Jew can truly feel at home, and as I listen to their deep feelings of isolation and alienation from American culture (feelings that I don't share), I begin to feel invisible once again — this time, as an American.

Invisibility is a symptom of my powerlessness. It forces me to recognize that I have little say over American domestic or foreign policy; that in the eyes of many Jews, I may never "count" as fully as my brothers; that to some feminists, my feminism is suspect as long as I cling to that "hopelessly patriarchal" and "clannish" religion, Judaism. As a Jew and as a woman, I am relegated, it seems, to the role of "other." Never mind that 51 percent of the American population is female or that, according to the rabbis, the lives of women are as valuable as those of men. When the authors of the Constitution defended the equality of men, they were not really talking about women (any more than they were talking about Jews, blacks, or poor people), and when the rabbis of the Talmud maintained that study and prayer are the means through which the Jew comes closest to God, they were issuing an invitation exclusively to men, since study and prayer were realms from which women were to be excused, if not excluded.

I am encouraged by the number of task forces on the equality of women that have recently been established within both the Jewish and the non-Jewish communities throughout the United States. I greeted with enthusiasm recent efforts to form a Jewish women's caucus within the feminist National Women' Studies Association. But the fact that such groups are necessary only serves to remind me of my powerlessness. The truth is that all three of my communities—the American, the Jewish, and the feminist—need to be pushed in order for my voice to be heard and for my vote to be counted.

Recently, I did a study of women's growing access to power within the Jewish community. The results were only slightly encouraging. Within Jewish organizations, outside of synagogue life, power remains overwhelmingly in the hands of men; there is little sign of improvement. In 1980, Chaim Waxman published an essay that focused on the impact of feminism on American Jewish communal institutions. His findings revealed that throughout the 1970s, there was little increase in the number of women serving as chief executive officers of Jewish organizations. In fact, he discovered, the only "category" of organizations in which significantly more women served as chief executive officers in 1979 than in 1969 was that of community relations: in 1979 there were 29.1 percent (seven out of twenty four), as opposed to 1969, where there were virtually none. Moreover, he noted,

> even within this category, we find that there was a greater increase in the percentage of women chief executive officers between 1969 and 1973, before the feminist movement could have had any great impact, than [between] 1973 and 1979.

As a result of those findings, Waxman concluded that "when viewed from the power perspective, it appears that the impact of feminism upon Jewish communal organizations has been negligible to virtually nil."

A 1981 survey on the status of women in Jewish communal services seems to confirm Waxman's assessment. While indicating that a significant number of women are involved in Jewish communal organizations, it reveals that the vast majority remain at low professional levels, appearing to have "very limited access to top executive and administrative positions." Reasons often cited for excluding women from these positions include the supposed reluctance of women to travel and to work in the evenings, their lack of training in management and business skills, and their reluctance to take managerial jobs. Yet as Naomi Levine, formerly the executive director of the American Jewish Congress (and as such, the first woman to become head of a major Jewish organization that was not a separate women's group), has noted, "these arguments are excuses to cover up a deep attitudinal reluctance to see women in new roles."

In the last five years, a number of major Jewish organizations have expressed a desire to discover new strategies for improving the position of women. But it may take another decade before significant numbers of women attain positions of communal leadership on the professional level. On the lay level, attaining positions of power may take even longer: first, because access to these positions seems to be directly related to personal wealth (using the argument that an individual will be a more efficient fund raiser if he or she is also a large contributor), and second, because the few women who have attained such positions do not seem to be feminists and have shown little if any interest in pressing for greater high-level involvement of women within their organizations. The Jewish Federation Council of Greater Los Angeles recently completed a study of women in federation and agency leadership roles. Concluding that women's opportunity to move into top leadership positions within the federation was limited, they recommended

> that the federation, applying the same standards to women and men, make a serious and sustained effort to involve greater numbers of women in leadership roles and committee chair positions.

While important changes may occur in Los Angeles as a result of this study, other Jewish communities have barely begun to acknowledge women's exclusion and have done little, if anything, to admit women to lay positions of influence and power.

Changes have come about more rapidly within the synagogue itself. Within the last ten years, growing numbers of women have become synagogue presidents and members of important decision-making committees. Moreover, within the synagogue service, women's participatory role clearly has expanded. In most Conservative congregations, women are now being counted in the *minyan* (the quorum of ten necessary for public worship); they are being called to the Torah; and, as of September 1984, they have been eligible to study for the conservative rabbinate at the movement's ordaining institution, the Jewish Theological Seminary of America. Within the Reform and Reconstructionist movements, where women have been ordained as rabbis for over ten years, new efforts are being made to gain acceptance for ordained women within congregations, and more generally, within Jewish communal institutions. In addition, while both movements have long accepted women, in theory if not in practice, as equal participants in the synagogue service, attempts are being made to create new liturgies that clearly reflect the inclusion of women as *Bnai Yisroel* ("children of Israel").

Within the Reform movement, efforts are also being made to create a more inclusive God-language. Some might argue that descriptions of God as Parent rather than Father, as Sovereign of Existence rather than King, either go too far or don't go far enough (I put myself in the latter camp). Nonetheless, I would maintain that *any* effort to depatriarchalize God is a good one. To me, there is no getting around the truth of Mary Daly's insight that as long as "God is in 'His' Heaven, ruling 'His' people," the position of women within

Judaism will continue to be subordinate to that of men. Moreover, as a Jew whose experience of the divine is of a being who is neither male nor female, I believe that to insist that male images are somehow more adequate than female images, that we can image God as "King of the Universe" but *not* as "Mistress of Heaven," is nothing short of idolatrous.

Although the Orthodox movement is far from ready to consider new images of God, Orthodox women have made great strides in the last ten years, moving metaphorically, and in some cases literally, from the back of the synagogue to separate but equal sides. Women's prayer groups have proliferated within the Orthodox community, religious education for women has greatly improved, and questions are at least being raised, if not answered, about expanding women's roles in the synagogue service.

Clearly, it is my feminism that leads me to recognize and acknowledge the sexism inherent not only within Judaism but also within American society. Yet in recognizing both racism and classism, my primary approach is not that of a feminist but rather that of a Jew. It is as a Jew that I feel commanded to take a stand against oppression, to seek justice and to work for its realization. It is as a Jew that I believe in the kinship of all human beings with God, and that as God's children, all of us have been created equal. Justice, as you know, forms the core of the prophetic message. This message is reiterated and strengthened by the rabbis who maintain that *Gemiluth Hasadim* ("deeds of loving kindness") are one of the three pillars on which the world rests. Although my childhood religious education was far from rigorous, I was deeply impressed by rabbinic sayings and teachings not to do unto others that which would be hateful to oneself, to love the stranger, to feed and clothe the poor, to work toward universal understanding and peace.

To be a good Jew, I learned, one needed to be a good

human being. Long after the Passover seder had ended, I would repeat my vow not to oppress others, remembering, in the words of the *Haggadah* (which tells the story of the Exodus) that I, too, had been a stranger in the land of Egypt. While, unfortunately, I'm not convinced that either the prophets or the rabbis equated a just world with a non-sexist society, I *am* convinced that racism and classism are antithetical to Jewish teachings and ideals.

Recently, however, the invisibility of Jews in discussions of racism and classism has led me to acknowledge that my powerlessness stems not only from my identification as a woman but also from my identity as a Jew. I have found that the unwillingness of many feminists and nonfeminists to name anti-Semitism as a form of racism reflects a refusal to take Jewish suffering seriously, a refusal to recognize that Jews, as individuals and as a people, are still being oppressed. Even more so, it reflects an unwillingness to acknowledge the hatred for Jews that still exists in our society, and a reluctance — albeit an understandable one — to confront the fact that anti-Semitism has been reflected in and perpetuated by the teachings of Christianity.

To a large extent, Christian anti-Semitism is rooted in the New Testament and in the writings of the church fathers. As Christianity separated itself from Judaism, as gentile Christianity triumphed over Jewish Christianity, and as the church gained official recognition from the Roman Empire, the church came to define itself more and more clearly in contradistinction to Judaism — the seeing church versus the blind synagogue, the sons of light versus the sons of darkness, believers versus unbelievers, members of a new covenant versus those foolishly clinging to the old. This view of Jews and Judaism was perpetuated by Martin Luther, whose virulent anti-Semitic attacks became part of his legacy to Lutheranism and, more generally, to Western Christianity.

In recent years, efforts have been made by the Catholic

church and by a number of American Protestant denominations to reevaluate Christian attitudes towards Judaism, including views of the relationship between the Jewish people and God. Yet even among feminist theologians, one often finds attitudes that claim to be "only anti-Judaism" but which are in fact anti-Semitic. As Annette Daum has noted, many have "all too often unintentionally but unquestioningly incorporated [into their theologies] the anti-Semitic prejudices of Christian male theologians of the past." Thus Jesus' feminism is contrasted with the sexism of the rabbis, and the liberating message of the gospel contrasted with the binding, oppressive nature of traditional Jewish law. Admittedly, the line between anti-Judaism and anti-Semitism is often a thin one. Yet as Elisabeth Schüssler Fiorenza reveals in her brilliant feminist reconstruction of early Christianity, *In Memory of Her*, to ignore the fact that the early Jesus movement reflected an authentic reforming impulse within Judaism itself — to contrast, in other words, early "Christians" with "Jews," when in fact the earliest Christians *were Jewish* — is to vilify Jewish history and to take a stance that is anti-Semitic in fact if not in intent.

Similarly, one frequently finds anti-Semitic remarks couched in more general criticisms of the state of Israel. All too often, critiques of Israeli policy become critiques of Jews. Those who equate Zionism with racism not only deny legitimate Jewish aspirations for a national homeland but also falsely equate the Zionist dream with the particular objectives of the current Israeli government. In 1983 at the National Women's Studies Association's conference in Columbus, Ohio, there were some who argued that if anti-Semitism were named as a form of fascism, it should be made clear that the word anti-Semitism implies hatred of all Semites, both Arabs and Jews. Although linguistically this argument may have merit, the fact is that those who advanced this argument did so out of a reluctance to single out

Jew-hatred—the common meaning of the word anti-Semitism—as something that the National Women's Studies Association should stand against. To accept this "new" definition of anti-Semitism, it was maintained, would reveal a commitment to seeking a just solution in the Middle East for Arabs and Jews. But those asking that the National Women's Studies Association take a stand against anti-Semitism as Jew-hating weren't talking about the Middle East. We were talking about the hatred for Jews that still exists in the world and that is as invidious as any other form of racism.

Finally, I feel invisible when I listen to discussions concerning Jews and money, when I hear jokes about Jewish greed and ignorant exclamations about Jewish control of the banks and the media in this country. Jews, as a group, *have* been economically successful in the United States. Yet as Gerald Krefetz reveals in his recently published study, Jews are also "among the least affluent groups in American society." According to Krefetz, more than 13 percent of all Jewish American households live below the poverty level, a figure comparable to, if not higher than, the national average. Yet the myth of Jewish wealth persists, the myth of the Jew as the successful capitalist, leading many to view any Jewish opposition to classism—or any Jew who admits to poverty—with some degree of suspicion.

Anti-Semitism, classism, and sexism converge most clearly in the images of the "Jewish American princess." Materialistic, spoiled, waiting for someone to take care of her as well and as lavishly as her father has, there seems to be little that is Jewish about this image, except for the princess' great desire for money—her insatiable greed. The fact that one "no longer needs to be Jewish to be a JAP" only reinforces the view that Jewish womanhood and conspicuous consumption go hand in hand.

As women of faith, we need to recognize the insidiousness of all images that dehumanize others. We need to recognize and name our power — a power that can arise only when we begin to work with one another toward our common and individual goals. We need to name our differences, without apologizing for them. Yet we also need to name — and to celebrate — all that brings us together.

PART THREE

A Dialogue
on Working Together
for Justice in the World

This dialogue is ably introduced by Eva Catafygiotu Topping, who thus adds yet another component to our dialogue — the voice of a Greek Orthodox scholar.

11

Working Together

Eva Catafygiotu Topping

In each historical situation faith has to be tested and demonstrated anew. Our faith, if it is truly alive, will address the complex and perilous times in which we find ourselves. The many issues and crises of our day will test our strength and purpose. In the conferences convened in 1980 and 1984, Women of Faith confronted the present historical situation, identifying the challenges and crises created by militarism and the threat of nuclear winter, by sexism and racism, and by social and economic injustice.

The five essays that follow in this section illustrate once again that diversity of religion, experience, and perspective need not divide us, and that unanimity of ideals and goals can be achieved. Three of the authors are Jewish, one Roman Catholic, and one Protestant. Being by birth Greek Orthodox, I represent another branch of Christianity, one that goes back to the very beginning of the church. Two of the authors are ordained women, one is a woman religious,

EVA CATAFYGIOTU TOPPING is a Greek Orthodox woman who has published articles concerning Byzantine hymnography in scholarly journals in the United States and elsewhere. She has also published articles on Greek-American history, American philhellenism, and the history of women in the Orthodox tradition.

the other two are laywomen active in their faith communities.

In her remarks Sister Ann Gillen highlights the need for coalitions. She correctly notes that forming coalitions is not easy. Indifference, ignorance, and unfavorable historical experience cause grave difficulties. Her plea is for us to understand what divides us and concentrate on what unites us.

Rabbi Sheila Peltz Weinberg addresses from a Jewish perspective two large issues: feminism and peace in the nuclear age. She pleads eloquently for the priority of life over death and for our commitment to activism in the cause of peace.

Inge Lederer Gibel describes anti-Semitism in the Soviet Union, the United States, the United Nations, and feminist organizations, explaining that anti-Zionism is a new garb for an old pathology.

The Reverend Elizabeth M. Scott identifies racism, classism, sexism, and ageism as four major evils that divide humankind. She names them "diseases in our domestic and international societies"; they are major causes of powerlessness.

Mimi Alperin comments on the rapidly changing patterns in women's lives and on the handicaps that women endure because of their sex. She points out that even in our "affluent" society, the feminization of poverty has become an acute problem.

The special focus on each paper notwithstanding, their authors agree on the major concerns of today's women of faith. A sense of urgency and crisis is apparent in all five essays. Their authors view militarism, racism (including anti-Semitism), sexism, and classism as life-destroying forces and as the causes of powerlessness, poverty, discrimination, and war. In the past decade more than forty wars have been fought on our small, fragile planet. Millions of our sisters and brothers are homeless and dying of starvation, while a few live in luxury and plenty.

The authors recognize the fact that social and economic evils have no national boundaries. The whole world, but especially the poor, must bear the crushing burden of top-heavy military budgets. No society is free from discrimination on the basis of race and sex. Finally, all these commentators agree that words are not enough. Faith is perfected in deeds: action to eradicate oppression, injustice, and violence, to transform the wilderness into a place good for all people.

Who can doubt that women of faith are faced with an enormous task of reconciling and healing? We have already made a beginning, by talking with one another in an effort to understand the differences that separate us and to discover the connections that unite us. Thus can we form a network that through further communication will expand nationally and internationally. Open and frank conversations are the necessary preliminaries to working together. In this way we can discover our common ideals and aspirations.

I am reminded of an old Greek proverb that I heard many times from my mother: "The one hand washes the other, the two together wash the face." This jewel of folk wisdom reflects the experience of villagers in a country whose people from earliest times have suffered poverty, war, and foreign rule. It is indeed a fact that had Greek villagers not helped one another, they would long ago have disappeared from the pages of history. Not even the proverb would have survived.

Today, the face that needs washing is no small homogeneous village of a few hundred people living in a community remote and separate from all others. Rather, it is our planet, over which is scattered a vast multiracial community that modern technology has joined into a global village whose inhabitants share a single fate. Therefore, many, many hands are required to wash from our face all forms of injustice, oppression, and violence. Only by working together in ever increasing numbers will we be able to save our global village from nuclear madness and extinction.

Inspired by faith, hope, and love, willing hearts and hands can build a new, just, and peaceful world order. Women of faith must join hands for this task.

12

A Rationale for
Coalition Building

Ann Gillen

Down through the centuries our Jewish, Christian, and
Muslim brothers have defined their separate paths in
divergent ways, possibly due to various political, historical,
and cultural factors, but also in opposition to one another
due to the "religious" wars of the past. However, I suspect
that in each age some women were good neighbors, meeting
at the wells to carry water or talking over the back fences
that the men had erected. But those were the exceptions.
Until recently, few if any opportunities have been available
to educated women of faith from various religious groups to
share their own insights and develop their own perspectives.

Take one example of such divergence: attitudes toward a
future life. Through belief in the resurrection of Jesus,
Christianity focused on happiness in a future life, while Judaism stressed the present life with greater vigor, describing
the Jewish hope for immortality in terms of good deeds done
in the present life and the continuity of a good name after

SISTER ANN GILLEN, S.H.C.J., is executive director of the National Interreligious Task Force on Soviet Jewry, an organization that works to
achieve freedom for Soviet Jews and other oppressed people.

death. Christians, looking forward to a better future life, stressed endurance, long-suffering, and patience, with the promise of eternal reward for such virtues. Life for Christians could be summed up as "putting up with one night in a bad hotel" (that is, enduring brief suffering now with an eternity of joy to come). Not so for Jews, who underscored humanity's responsibility to *improve* the hotel, not simply to endure its privations.

The analogy of the hotel paints the situation in very broad strokes but the result of such divergent views is evident, I hope. Our value systems do not always mesh easily, whether in a conversation or in a major crisis. Suppose you are sent to prison unjustly; if you want to be freed, you are probably far better off if you have the support of Jewish friends; they will do something about it with prophetic vigor. Christians are more likely to pray that you will become a saint in prison. (However, this is not to imply that the apparent tension between the seen and the unseen casts doubt upon the power of prayer.)

Nonetheless, when there is a death in the family, you are more likely to find the Christian view of a future family reunion more consoling. My question is this: Why must we continue this division of the heritage of faith, the division of life and death, time and eternity?

The Greek analogy, like the Semitic parable, makes a single statement, throwing one small ray of light on a given subject. Another analogy that may help us understand our differences somewhat is that of the orange. Take the outer skin of the Jewish orange: the layers representing people, religion, and culture are almost one, so that Jews tend to be "thin skinned." Christians, however, tend to be "thick skinned," somewhat fragmented by layers of different races, nations, and denominations. At the heart of the orange, however, we find our common humanity and our shared womanhood. So, it is good for us to probe below the surfaces for inner meaning.

In a sense, this probing is one of the key purposes of our dialoguing together. Our speaking, listening, and sharing have thrown many single rays of light on the central reality — or should I say possibility? — of our sisterhood. As a result, we hope that each one sees more clearly where we have come from, where we are, and where we can go *together*. We do not seek to "triumph" over one another; we seek to find the truth of our common existence.

While our conversations have been marked by civility and much consensus, there are still undoubtedly some issues on which we disagree. I hope that this conference will inspire us to read more about one another's positions on these issues and also to have further dialogue with local groups.

I hope, too, that we have some determination to implement programs and to build coalitions on the issues concerning which we can cooperate. I happen to be involved in one such issue, the struggle for religious liberty and/or emigration for Jews, Christians, and Muslims in the Soviet Union and Eastern Europe. Frequently I am asked why I, as a Roman Catholic sister, should be involved in the cause of Soviet Jewry? And I outline what I learned in Catholic schools about Jews and Judaism.

Pius XI wrote an encyclical that did not stop the Holocaust, but that did turn the direction of history for Catholics by stating that "spiritually we are all Semites." Pius XII did not, more probably could not, have saved the Jews in the concentration camps, but he urged biblical scholars to return to the sources — people, land, and language — if they wished to know what the Word of God means. This scholarship was part of the foundation of the Second Vatican Council and thus brought about profound changes in church life. Pope John XXIII exemplified these changes in his own personal expression of our common humanity. Thus, at ten-year intervals in my lifetime, papal statements brought Catholics closer to cooperation with Jews, until finally guidelines were written urging that we "work willingly together in areas of common social concern."

As I matured I wondered what actions had been evoked by these statements. The encyclicals were written for the whole Roman Catholic church. Why was there not more response, and much earlier response? In addition to the implications of the analogies of hotel and orange, there was as well the pervasive and pathetic plaint, "What can I do? I'm only one person." At some point along the line, I decided to try to see what one person can do. I soon discovered that I was not working alone. There were others who were also trying. Hasn't that been your experience, too? I bless the memory of the many persons who have inspired me. Let me name three of them.

The first is Cornelia Connelly, founder of the Society of the Holy Child. She was a 19th-century American woman, wife of a Protestant minister and mother of five children, whose life was dramatically changed after their conversion to Roman Catholicism and her husband's subsequent desire to become a priest. In the 19th-century that vocation of her husband practically necessitated that she become a sister.

Tragically, after his ordination and her foundation of our religious society, her husband changed his mind and eventually sued her for the restoration of his conjugal rights. Despite the suffering of her personal family life, or perhaps due to those tangled relationships, she founded a larger family and turned the minds of her sisters to an even larger family by telling us that one of our goals was "to meet the wants of the age." In our Vatican II renewal, then, all we had to do was ask ourselves, "What age are we talking about?"

My second inspiring person is Sargent Shriver, still very much alive and active, who sent our group this message when the National Interreligious Task Force on Soviet Jewry was formed in Chicago in 1972: "It's too late to help the Jews who died in the Holocaust but it's not too late to help the Soviet Jews, and it's not too late to try to turn the direction of history." Turning the direction of history? A monumental task, surely, if long overdue!

Third, I want to mention the late Saul Alinsky, Jewish community organizer, whom I met, strangely enough, at a Catholic liturgical conference on liberation theology. Alinsky said, "If you can organize and activate even 2 percent of a group and they are educated and willing to be articulate, you can change the direction of history."

Since then I've seen it happening. Who can't find 2 percent out there who are ready and willing to respond? If a small group accepts responsibility and exerts leadership, others are willing to follow. In the past decade, 10 percent of Soviet Jews have been allowed to emigrate. That's still not enough, but it is a miracle when one considers that few, if any, had been able to leave the Soviet Union before.

The task force of which I am executive director is one example of a small but effective coalition. The National Interreligious Task Force on Soviet Jewry — a group of Catholics, Protestants, and Jews seeking to help both Jews and Christians in the Soviet Union and Eastern Europe — was founded in 1972 by the American Jewish Committee (AJC) and the National Catholic Conference for Interracial Justice (NCCIJ). Since the early 1900s, when the AJC was founded after a pogrom in Kishinev, it has been concerned about the international dimensions of anti-Semitism. The NCCIJ was established by Catholics to combat racism in the United States. Members of both groups had participated in the American civil-rights struggle of the sixties, and they were concerned about the human-rights struggle of the seventies.

In the work of the task force, there seemed to be a natural convergence of issues into a common agenda, as well as an evolution from a national to an international perspective. What was begun as a work of education and liberation became also a work of reconciliation, as we worked together to free prisoners of conscience. Our work had national dimensions as we formed local groups in various parts of the United States, urging their members to appeal to national religious and political leaders for their cooperation. The work of the task force has also had international dimensions: we have supported the United Nations Universal Declaration of Human Rights, which affirms the right to emigrate (article thirteen) and the right to freedom of religion (article eighteen); and we have sent delegations to the Belgrade and Madrid conferences to lobby the national delegates in their review of the Helsinki Final Act, an agreement that contained important human-rights provisions.

At Belgrade, the United States representative criticized the Soviets for their failure to allow freedom of emigration to Soviet Jews. The Soviets pointed to the case of the Wilmington Ten as an American failure to honor human rights. Later, the task force was invited to help plan the first official United States State Department conference on human rights. We insisted that the meeting include seminars not only on the failures of other nations but also on five cases of human-rights problems in the United States: the Wilmington Ten, Native American Indians, women, Hispanics, and Asian-Americans. These groups were all invited to present their cases at the State Department conference. There I expressed the hope that some day a similar conference will be held in the Kremlin with Sakharov, Orlov, Scharansky, and numerous other prisoners of conscience presenting their grievances, their stories of the Soviet Union's failure to honor its own laws as well as international agreements.

Now let's turn to the importance — the problems and the potential — of forming interreligious coalitions of women.

Let us review what happened at the 1980 United Nations Conference on Women, in Copenhagen.

I went to Copenhagen with some experience of international dialogue about human rights, expecting to meet other women to continue this discussion. I was not uncritical of the United States, but I was well aware that the Soviets had failed in countless ways to honor international human-rights provisions, particularly in regard to Soviet Jews, and had orchestrated anti-Semitic propaganda campaigns against the emigration movement.

The Copenhagen conference was a multi-faceted eighteen-day experience. At the Bella Center, eighteen hundred official delegates and two hundred observers from 145 states heard lengthy monologues for almost a week of reports and greetings. From the data gathered since the earlier Mexico City conference, we learned that women comprise one-half of the world's population and one-third of the world's labor force, work two-thirds of the work hours, take home one-tenth of the world's income, and own less than one percent of the world's property. However, since the official conference was controlled by the votes of the Soviets and other Marxists, along with Arab and other third-world countries, the women's agenda was to be used as another means of excoriating Israel. Now Zionism was to be added to the list of the world's evils in its own right, not simply as a form of racism, as the Mexico City conference had previously declared it to be.

However, I still thought that women might be able to meet and exchange views at the "non-government organizations" meetings that took place at Almager University. Some eight thousand women and a few men shared in a ten-day avalanche of information about women everywhere, choosing among more than 150 workshops daily. Some 1,250 journalists shuttled back and forth from official to unofficial meetings, covering walkouts and sit-ins, demonstrations and marches. East-West tensions were evident everywhere. Palestinian Leila Khaled grabbed the headlines early: the former hijacker proclaimed that she would speak to Israel only with weapons, not words. Danish Jewish women circulated a petition calling on Arab women to join them in a common search for peace. Danish Christians and Jews held a demonstration for Israel together; reminding us of World War II, when Denmark was the only European nation to save its Jews. With Danish Jews and Western Christian women attending the conference, I participated in a demonstration for Soviet Jewish refusenik and prisoner Ida Nudel.

Among the groups of women who wished to tell their story were the Ukrainians. With other religious and ethnic groups in the USSR, Ukrainians oppose Soviet efforts to Russify their culture, to Sovietize their mentality, to replace their religious roots with scientific atheism. Ukrainian prisoners are often given very long sentences. One former prisoner, Nina Strokata, wished to speak about Ukrainian prisoners, especially her husband, who had a thirty-year sentence. The Ukrainian women invited me to join them in giving a human-rights workshop at Almager University: they planned to have a general discussion after we told about the Ukrainian and Jewish human-rights problems in the USSR. However, such was not to be.

Soon after Nina Strokata had described the United Nations human-rights provision and had begun to speak about the oppression suffered by Ukrainians, a chorus of complaints interrupted the speaker. Three women in various parts of the room apparently agreed that they had heard enough from the speaker. They wanted to speak about their sufferings, too. Rapidly the meeting degenerated into a shouting match of women saying yes (let the Ukrainian speaker finish) and no (let other women speak). An outside mediator was called in to make peace. After various attempts at persuasion, she proposed that each woman be allowed to speak for three minutes. Thus, Nina Strokata and the Ukrainians who organized the meeting would lose their opportunity. Not content with that, the Arab women who were the trio of dissenters announced that they had decided (without any apparent consultation in the room) to give their three minutes to the Soviet delegate from Ukraine, who would give the correct version of the human-rights situation there. We had been outmaneuvered by three women who looked as if they came from different continents and spoke for different constituencies. Their maneuvers revealed that they had come armed with a plan to silence Ukrainian criticism of the Soviet Union. The workshop broke up, with many refusing to listen to the Soviet official.

Later I was not surprised to see that these same three women traveled to and from the meetings in a bus with others from their group called Women's International Democratic Federation. When I saw the trio enter the room where the Israeli Women's seminar was to be held, I knew we would have trouble there, too. They tried again but were less successful. Perhaps the Israeli women were better prepared because of the previous experience. Perhaps the opposition had another power play in mind. Outside the workshop, anti-Israel demonstrators came shouting down the corridor. Jewish women began to panic, looking for some escape exit. For them, pogroms are still a frightfully alive memory and terrorist attacks an enduring threat. (Most Christians have not really studied church history and know even less of synagogue history. For such, I recommend Father Edward Flannery's *Anguish of the Jews* and Sister Suzanne Noffke's filmstrip *Troubled Brotherhood*, two Catholic efforts to bridge this terrible gap).

Women had great difficulty focusing the attention of the conference on the evils of sexism. The male-dominated mechanism directed by the Soviet coalition was bent on spotlighting the evils of imperialism (excluding any focus on

Afghanistan), colonialism (excluding Eastern Europe), racism (sabotaging the United States resolution condemning racism), and Zionism (favoring all liberation movements except for the Jewish struggle for survival).

Western women, particularly those from the United States, found themselves surrounded by a chorus of critics, embroiled in an East-West ideological controversy. The Soviet thesis was expounded as follows: property is at the root of women's problems; they have even been treated as men's property. Therefore, join the national liberation movements against imperialism, colonialism, and so forth, and not only will you be freed as women, but also your fathers, husbands, brothers, and sons will be freed, too. Western feminists, in contrast, spoke of the patriarchal structures of society as the main problem, and finally, one Russian feminist, Natalia Malachovskaya, arrived in Copenhagen to voice agreement. An editor of a Soviet feminist publication, Malachovskaya declared that after a revolution and sixty years of being without property, Soviet women are still enslaved by the patriarchal structure and customs in much the same fashion Western feminists describe.

These Soviet feminists have their own characteristics and goals. In 1980, they numbered only thirty and had published very little, yet so formidable was their voice that three of the editors were deported that same summer. Malachovskaya was confident that the feminist movement would continue to grow quickly in the Soviet Union. Ironically, while this Soviet critic was not even allowed to have an official press conference inside the Bella Center, ex-hijacker Leila Khaled was an invited guest who was even able to lead a "walkout" when Mrs. Gihan Sadat spoke to the delegations. Later in a Copenhagen hotel, however, Natalia was able to tell her story.

Natalia stated that Soviet women in her group decided that it is the patriarchal structure of society which is the root of women's problems. They have no property in the USSR but they do have a strong patriarchy. If Western women had been able to hear her, they would have applauded her censure of patriarchal problems.

As a woman of faith, I was interested in this powerless woman whose views had so challenged the powerful Soviet system. I asked if she was Russian Orthodox? No, she had chosen to be a Czechoslovakian Catholic. Impressed by the courage of Charter 77 members, she had opted to join them even at a great distance. Other members of her group were Baptist and Jewish. An interesting Women of Faith group: in the Soviet Union, small in number, powerless in many ways, yet empowered by their common faith despite diversity!

Each group, Catholic, Protestant, Jewish, and Muslim, passes on its own tradition, its stories of sufferings and triumphs, its traditions and customs, largely to its own children. Women play a large part in this story telling. They might have had a unique opportunity to share these stories with other groups and persons in Copenhagen. In my opinion and from my perspective, Western groups, including those from the United States and Israel, came ready to dialogue; the opposing coalition came determined not to dialogue but to dominate — both at the official meetings and at the Almager nongovernmental-organizational meetings. They came better prepared for that purpose, with their "goon squad" tactics. So, Copenhagen was a painful experience in power and powerlessness. As a woman of faith, I shared in the frustration of women who saw their hopes for the agenda subverted. In a special way I shared in the powerlessness of Jewish and Ukrainian women, both minorities scorned by the powerful at Copenhagen. Why were these two groups singled out for such opposition at Copenhagen? Let us consider each group briefly.

Needless to say, anti-Semitism antedates the Soviet Union by millennia. Jews have suffered anti-Semitism throughout the history of Western Christendom and even before. In Russia, they suffered under the Czars and might well have hoped for relief through the Revolution. Both Lenin and Stalin signed a document pledging a new policy toward national groups, including the "abolition of all national religious restrictions" and "the free development of national minorities and ethnic groups inhabiting the territory of Russia." History has shown that such promises were interpreted (and subverted) within the overreaching goals of Soviet leaders: to Russify and to Sovietize all ethnic and cultural groups, and to replace religious traditions with those of scientific atheism.

Religious Jews and Zionists have been targets of attack from the early days of the Revolution. In July 1919, a Communist party resolution called for the suppression of the Zionist party because it "strengthened among the backward Jewish masses the influence of clericalism and nationalist attitudes." The *Kaheillah* communal organization and Hebrew, the religious language, were banned. Synagogues were closed along with the churches, which lost at least four-fifths of their members as well as an equally substantial proportion of their religious freedom.

Rather than rejecting Czarist anti-Semitism, the Soviet leaders have continued it, borrowing from Nazi propaganda and expanding upon it. Research on one such vicious document from the late 1960s revealed its origin to be a police gazette published in Cairo at a time when Egypt's propaganda apparatus was headed by Johannes Von Leers, a Nazi fugitive and former associate of Joseph Goebbels, Hitler's propaganda minister.

A later survey of Soviet publications (all state controlled) stated that in 1981 approximately 1,814 negative anti-Jewish items were printed in Soviet media, about eight items per day. There was not one single positive reference to Jews, Judaism, Israel, and the like. Instead, Jews were presented as aggressive, dangerous people. On prime-time Soviet television, Soviet Jewish emigration leaders have been identified as disloyal persons or CIA agents.

Recently, a committee of Sovietized Jews was created in the USSR to echo the offical view that emigration is closed, all Jews have left who desired to emigrate, and discrimination against Jews does not exist in the USSR. However, Vladimir Solovyov, Soviet historian and journalist, warns that "Soviet Jews find themselves in a trap from which there is no way out internally, that only international intervention will work."

Only international intervention will work? Our challenge is to find intervention that *will* work. The Soviets maintain that we merely define human rights differently. The West affirms personal and civil liberties, but it has grave unemployment problems among its peoples. The Soviets have full employment, affirming collective social and economic rights. For the uninformed, this sounds plausible, perhaps.

But the Ukrainian experience reveals the falsity of this view of human rights. Recall that in 1983 the Ukrainian people remembered the fiftieth anniversary of the Ukrainian famine, a man-made famine engineered by Stalin to quell resistance in the Ukraine and to silence dissent there. The Ukrainian harvest was taken from the people who raised the grain, and seven million Ukrainians starved to death. Pavel Litvihoff points out that, lacking civil and political freedom, the Ukrainians had no way to ask the outside world to send help. They still had the right and duty to work—full employment; but denied their harvests and adequate food, they did not have the basic human right to life. Like the Jews, Ukrainians today remember what happened to their people. They seek redress as well as remembrance.

Jews and Ukrainians had much in common at Copenhagen: they were both targeted by the Soviets to be censured and silenced. One can understand how the Soviets might fear the stories of groups that had suffered so much.

What can we learn from all this? We can see that the divisiveness of the religiously and ethnically oriented wars of previous centuries has now escalated to worldwide economic and political struggle. As women begin their own struggle to be freed from bondage, whether because they have been treated as property and sex objects or whether they have been dominated in patriarchal structures or both, they will need to be wary of the explosive legacy of earlier conflicts. For example, I saw one Jewish woman in tears because Dorothy Height was the delegate who had to withdraw the United States resolution condemning racism. We all know that Dorothy Height has spent her life struggling to overcome that evil. Dorothy Height must have been in anguish at that moment but she knew that the Soviet block was ignoring the American warning that amendments to the resolution would not be accepted; the opposition was bent on using this resolution to condemn Zionism again. Dorothy Height's action indicated our nation's continued commitment to the survival of Israel. I think that we should be just as aware of the legitimate self-interests of blacks and of other racial, religious, and ethnic groups.

At Copenhagen a Jewish woman seeking support from an ethnic group for Israel, was dismayed to have a friend deter her with this remark, "You're not going to talk with that fascist?" Is there not a tyranny of labels? How can we build coalitions if, because of problems of the past, we dismiss the possibility of dialogue with whole groups? Is it not possible that some persons in every group may be part of that precious 2 percent that we need to change the direction of history? Do we not have enough problems in the present to claim all our energies?

In times of economic setbacks such as we have today, scapegoating is a popular social outlet for stress. I recall being horrified to learn from the study of sociology that as the price of cotton fell in the Old South, the number of lynchings increased. Today we share the anger and anxiety of the Jewish community at the upsurge of anti-Semitism in many lands. This is not the time to withdraw into ourselves as persons or as groups. This is the time to reach out our hands to one another, to build bridges rather than walls and fences. Our sisterhood may be visionary now; it must become an effective reality.

The bonding of women is a fast-growing reality because our roots in bondage are all too apparent for those who have eyes to see or ears to hear. On a Chicago bus an elderly black woman sank into a seat beside me, murmuring, "That bus driver was so considerate; she waited for me to sit down. We women have to hang together. The men do." In a sense, that said it all. But the roots of our problems are centuries old and our awareness has just begun. If we are to make progress in our lifetimes, we must set priorities and cooperate on issues where we can agree.

For example, we hear that a spate of sexually violent films featuring attacks on women and female dismemberment is about to be released. One critic lamely concluded that these films might be a way of "venting male aggressiveness." Is there not the greater likelihood that these films will result in more crimes of violence against women? What are we going to do about it? Recently a judge spoke to a group of social workers and remarked that he would enjoy "a garden-variety rape" case that would give him some vicarious pleasure. History was made, not by his remark, but by the fact that his listeners did *not* laugh. We need to continue our dialogue to devise solutions for such problems.

As women of faith, we need to continue to learn when to laugh and when not to laugh; when to be angry and how to be angry in such a way that we can change the systems that oppress us. Some women need to learn that they have a right to be angry; some men need to learn that women have a reason to be angry.

Will our brothers stand in our way or come to our aid? Can we count on their help in our coalition? Again, look for the 2 percent and you will find them. In Copenhagen, I met a young man, an engineer, a husband and father of two children; he was also wearing a skirt. Not a kilt, a long skirt. He explained that he is a "masculist" bent on freeing males from their restrictive rule just as feminists seek the same for women. The "masculist" group has "flexism" on its agenda, a campaign to change business hours so that both husbands and wives can have careers and share the duties and joys of being father and mother.

A "masculist" philosophy maintains that it is easier for the alleged inferior sex to wear the clothing of the "superior" sex than for males to begin wearing skirts! I said to my young "masculist" friend in Copenhagen, "You are a brave man." Few women wish their husbands to be equally brave. Prophets sometimes do strange things to make us think; they're not always easy to live with. Society does not easily understand what they are trying to tell us by their actions. They remind us that there will be still more change, more confrontation, and (we hope) more cooperation in the future. As women of faith, let us carry on our work with that reminder, with better understanding, and with greater hope.

13

Judaism, Feminism, and Peace in the Nuclear Age

Sheila Peltz Weinberg

We are all living in fear, and understandably so. Signals of distress for our planet and the human species flash before us. Expenditures soar to trillions of dollars. The more security is preached, the less secure we feel. More sophisticated and more deadly weapons are being transferred around the globe daily.

Since the beginning of the Reagan era our despair has increased, and with good reason. We have been to Three Mile Island. We have seen the end of détente, the failure to ratify the SALT II treaty, deadlock after deadlock in disarmament negotiations, the beginning of first strike cruise missile and Pershing II deployment in Europe, and a military budget bloated with space-war super-nuclear weaponry.

I remember hearing years ago that the only means to end war and national rivalries on earth would be an invasion by Mars. Then we would respond to the common threat from

SHEILA PELTZ WEINBERG is the rabbi of Beth Am Israel, a Reconstructionist synagogue in Penn Valley, Pennsylvania. She is active in various feminist and peace organizations.

outside and develop earthling solidarity and cooperation. Well, in a very real sense the invasion from Mars has occurred. Mars, the ancient god of war, holds the planet in his palm. In 1980 the Republican national platform said, "We will build toward a sustained defense expenditure sufficient to close the gap with the Soviets, and ultimately reach the position of military superiority that the American people demand." Is this really what the American public wants? The last few years have not demonstrated this to be true. In a Harris survey taken in September 1983, 77 percent of those polled favored a congressional resolution calling upon the United States to negotiate a nuclear freeze with the Soviet Union under which both sides would ban the future production, storage, and use of their nuclear weapons.

Indeed, while Mars rattles his sword louder and louder, new ways of thinking and acting *are* spreading across the nation. Americans from many walks of life — in professional and business groups, labor-union committees, established religious organizations, environmental groups, neighborhood and women's associations — are moving beyond their despair, anger, and confusion to search for their own basis of real security. There are already more than fifty nationwide peace organizations and thousands of regional and local ones. These individuals and groups do not have the answer to despair. They do not know the way out of the woods. But they know that they and the world cannot continue along the same path, and that together people can search for a new way into the future.

When I confronted my own fear, pain, and anguish, I knew there had to be a response other than the immobility of anxiety and despair or the deadness of denial. I went to the personal and collective identity-value base that is nearest to me. I reached out to the traditions and communities that were closest to me in language and could offer me the most nurturance: I looked toward my identity as a Jew and as a woman. This, I believe, is the common process that has caused the growth of myriad particular groups, all of whom share the universal search for world peace and a new paradigm of human life on this earth.

I would like to share with you today more tentative thoughts about how Judaism and feminism nourish and encourage working for disarmament, and how these seemingly disparate approaches to reality can stimulate and enhance the personal and collective pursuit of peace.

Historically, both women and Jews have lived the role of victim, of objectified "other." From that special vantage point as stereotyped and oppressed, we understand that true liberation consists in affirming ourselves without objectifying the opponent. The arms race feeds on a mentality of objectification. From earliest childhood we are reared on images of the Russian people and their leaders as warmongers and madmen. We are still being urged to believe in a win-lose model of international relations that mirrors interpersonal relations in traditional hierarchical societies. Feminism introduces a model of participation and empowerment as opposed to competition and absolute individualism. In the nuclear age, the winners versus the losers, the good guys versus bad guys, the Wild West macho-cowboy mentality is totally obsolete. It never functioned very well. But in today's world, encircled by fifty thousand nuclear warheads, the idea of "winning" a nuclear war is suicidal thinking.

It is true that not all people who experience oppression develop an ethic that is opposed to oppression. Such an ethic, however, is central to most feminist theory and practice, and I believe it is absolutely integral to Judaism. The central historic event in Jewish life is the Exodus from Egypt, the liberation of a rag-tag horde of slaves who at the beginning of the story are quite unaware of their own oppression. Ultimately they become sufficiently empowered to be partners with the Creator of the Universe in a very demanding and ethical covenant. The eternal message of the Exodus is not to glory in the defeat of the oppressors or wait until they become the losers and we the victors. The essence of the teaching is a rejection of master-slave power relations. The main message is that whichever way you turn in a relationship of exploitation or objectification, you lose.

There is a metaphor in Jewish prayers that is difficult to relate to as a democrat, never mind as a feminist. Yet I have pondered it for a long while, and I believe that in its own dated language it expresses a fundamental truth about power relations. The metaphor is that of God as King. It means that the earthly power of kings and states must be limited. This metaphor is a cry against the assumption of absolute power, which is exactly what underlies bloated defense budgets and recycled cold-war rhetoric. As we experience empowerment as women and Jews, we tap into the power of divine sovereignty, which forces us to challenge the assumptions of the nations who play God.

Judaism and feminism share a radical alternative vision of the world as well as a basic optimism that change is possible — not easy and not fast, but possible. Jewish images of the alternative future abound. We call it the Messiah. We mean world peace. The Hebrew prophets are the most articulate in expressing the vision. The Sukkah is an adumbration of the security to come, based on inner strength.

Rabbi Levi said:

> Beloved is peace, for all the blessings end with "peace." In the recitation of the Shema, God spreads the tabernacle of peace; the tefilah ends with "peace," the priestly blessing ends with "peace" — "and give thee peace." (Deut. Raba V, 15)

Rabbi Simeon B. Halafta said:

> See how beloved is peace; when God sought to bless Israel He

found no other vessel which could comprehend all the blessings wherewith [She] would bless them, save peace. How do
we know it? For it is said, the Lord will give strength unto
[Her] people; the Lord will bless His people with peace."
(Psalm 39:11; Deut. Raba V, 15)

Peace may be the vessel of blessing, but Judaism as well as
feminism is marked by a profound understanding of the in-
terconnectedness of life. Rosemary Reuther discusses her alternative vision:

> We seek an alternative power principle of empowerment in
> community rather than power over and disabling others.
> Such enabling in community is based on a recognition of the
> fundamental connectedness of life, of men and women,
> blacks and whites, Americans and Nicaraguans, Americans
> and Russians, humans and the nonhuman community of ani-
> mals, plants, air, and water. Nobody wins unless all win.[1]

Awareness of the interconnections of life comes from the
experience of women who feel life moving and pulsing within and know from inside the rhythms of creation and
change. We also affirm the truth that the same life-denying
violence that flees from its own insecurity is found in the
rapist, in the wife beater, and in the insatiable urge for
security through more and more and more firepower.

Judaism's deepest insights concern the consciousness of the
creation of the world by a purposeful and loving creator. All
and everything is related by virtue of our common male/
female parent. On Rosh Hashanah, the Jewish New Year,
two themes predominate. First, it is the birthday of the
world—our sensitivity to creation is aroused. The second
theme is a renewal of faith and commitment to growth on a
personal and collective level. Our awareness of creation in
all its wondrous reciprocity fills us with a sense of mutual
responsibility. This leads us forward as individuals and

groups to fulfill our unique and important part in the web of life.

Indeed, Judaism, like feminism, is a political theory and a path that holds life to be the highest value. Women and Jews are, we might say, obsessed with life, obsessed with survival. This passion is now desperately needed. Judaism and feminism see not only murder, but also hunger, poverty, ignorance, psychological manipulation, and lack of meaningful work as forms of violence that destroy life and the human image. My own sense of God comes from this awareness. As Mordecai Kaplan taught, God is found in the emergent faith in the worth of human personality. He wrote:

> The regenerative tendency in humankind is asserting itself in a deepened respect for that incommunicable and untransferable individuality in the human being which is the point of reference of everything that is sacred and beautiful . . . it is conferring rights upon the woman, the child, the disinherited, the oppressed. It is the inspiration behind the striving for equitable distribution of opportunities. By understanding all that is implied in human worth the Jew can gain deeper insight into her own spiritual heritage.[2]

Our faith in God is democratic and human-centered. We feel we are part of a process of raising the value of life. We search for God within ourselves, within the intricate patterns of life. Our commitment to work toward disarmament is a manifestation of that faith. Our God is not an external authority, but the energy that helps us move out to one another, share our dreams and fears, encourage and validate ourselves beyond the temptations of despair, anxiety, and denial. As Jews and as women we know that denial makes us powerless and passive. The Jewish ritual of grief and mourning is an excellent example of moving through deep feelings and reaching past those feelings into an affirmation of life. We recite a special mourner's prayer that begins *yitgadal viyitkadash sh'may raba* ("magnified and sanctified may the name of the Creator be").

So far we have described the value base that underlies our willingness to explore new ways of thinking and acting that can nourish life in all its fullness and remove from our world the specter of nuclear holocaust. In Judaism we speak of the Torah as the tree of life. The Torah is a term that cannot be translated into any other language. It has far too many connotations. It embodies the alternative vision that we spoke about earlier. But it is more than a vision. It is a blueprint, too. It suggests that one must translate visions through two fundamental methods, law and education. This, then, is what the peace movement, women's movement, and Judaism are seeking to do. There are many ways where I imagine these three spokes of my identity meshing. Let me name just three of these ways.

First, I think there is a good chance that many other women who have already seen the connection between peace activism and feminism would be nurtured by feeling connected to the deep roots of their Jewish heritage. I had some experience last summer bringing a little bit of Sabbath to the Women's Encampment for a Future of Peace and Justice, in Seneca Falls. The Jewish women were receptive. Every bit of support helps when one is struggling against the overwhelming power of Mars! It is healing to be affirmed by your ancestral faith, particularly when that faith has not yet been integrated into your adult being.

Second, I would like to see Jewish women's organizations, which have mobilized great talent, energy, compassion, and funds on behalf of Israel and world Jewry, become connected to the women's peace movement and to overall disarmament work. Even in the Republican party 21 percent more men than women support Reagan's armament policy; and most women in Jewish organizations identify with the goals of national and local peace organizations. These women should be encouraged to join coalitions in their communities and to see disarmament as *the universal issue* without which their particular commitments will be meaningless.

Third, I would like to see Jewish women become more active and use their gifts for leadership to encourage the overall Jewish community's participation in peace activism and related areas. Women activists who see the broader picture perhaps could play a significant role in challenging the inwardness that has marked the Jewish communal agenda in recent years.

Two tasks remain to be mentioned. First, there are many ways to demonstrate the connections between feminism and peace. It is incumbent upon *us* to invent new, powerful means of communicating this message, both to people who are like us and to those who are not. Our women-of-faith conferences have been models: there are many people of different classes, religions, and races, — or of the opposite sex — with whom we need to communicate about connections and alternative visions, without arousing suspicion, fear, or resentment.

Second is an equally difficult task: we need to explore with each other ways of infusing other peace and religious organizations with the best values of the feminist non-hierarchical perspective. The women's movement is discovering and has discovered different ways of doing things that need to be taught — in ways that "others" can learn.

To the extent that both of these things — making connections and teaching feminist perspective — are happening, they need to be made more conscious, sharper, and clearer.

I would like to close with a story related in the Talmud (Brachot 10a). There were once some highwaymen in the neighborhood of Rabbi Meir who caused him a great deal of trouble. The rabbi accordingly prayed that they should die. His wife, B'ruriah, said to him:

How do you allow such a prayer to be permitted? It is written: "Let sins [*hataim*] cease." Is it written: "sinners" (*hot'im*)? No. It is written "sins" (*hataim*). Further look at the end of the verse (Psalm 104:35), "and let the wicked men be no more." Since the sins will cease, there will be no more wicked men. Rather, pray for them that they repent, and there will be no more wicked.

He did pray for them, and they repented.

Perhaps it is no accident that it was a woman, surely one of the very few female sages whose words were recorded, who makes the distinction between one's being and one's behavior. This is a polemic against any and all oppression based on objectification and stereotyping. It is also a commitment to faith in the goodness of human life and the possibility of return and renewal. In this time of danger and fear, I find sources of courage and hope in being a Jewish woman. I pray that I can share this Torah with my sisters and brothers of all religions, so that together we can pursue peace.

NOTES

1. "Feminism and Peace," *Christian Century*, 100, no. 25 (31 Aug. 1983).

2. *The Religion of Ethical Nationhood* (New York: Reconstructionist Press, 1970), p. 198.

14

Anti-Semitism and Its Role
in International Politics

Inge Lederer Gibel

Two images haunted me as I thought about and wrote this essay. The first was of a little girl I never knew, Anne Frank, whose fate I escaped by the slightest chance of history, and about whom I think often. With her childhood faith, as reflected in her famous diary, I, too, want to believe that most people are basically good, and that one day there will be a better world. If she had survived, if she could see the world of today, forty years after she died of typhus and starvation at Bergen-Belsen, would she still believe?

But even more than the spirit of Anne Frank, my father's

INGE LEDERER GIBEL, a Jew who combines aspects of Orthodox and Reform practices, was for many years a member of the Reconstructionist Movement and its founding synagogue. She formerly served as program associate in interreligious affairs for the American Jewish Committee and was the founding member of the New York–based Task Force of Women of Faith in the 80s. President of Americans for Progressive Israel, an officer of Breira, editor of the New York NAACP *Voice*, senior staff consultant to the largest American Jewish delegation in Nairobi in 1985, Ms. Gibel has published articles in *Harper's*, *The Village Voice*, and *The Amsterdam News*. She is now living in Israel, and frequently writes concerning the Middle East and interreligious affairs for Christian and Jewish publications.

spirit is very much with me, and this paper is dedicated to
his memory. Robert Lederer — Israel ben Gabriel — was tak-
en home by God on 31 March 1983, at last reunited with his
beloved mother and sister. In the central trauma of his life
and my childhood, I watched him embrace my grandmother and aunt for the last time. He left them to save his wife
and children from the brutal end whose name we did not yet
know. Still he was desperate with concern for those dear
gentle souls for whom no visas could be obtained, for whom
America's doors were closed, and who perished in the bow-
els of the beast during what has become known as the Holocaust, at Theresienstadt and Auschwitz.

After that cold and bitter night in 1938 on a railway platform in Vienna, I don't think my father was ever, for a
moment, without the anguish of that parting and the burden of that terrible choice. But as he taught me by example
as well as words, never to forget and never to stand by and
let it happen again, he also taught me, more than anyone in
my life, to love all humankind as well as the Jewish people,
to be concerned with the suffering of all God's children, not
just our own. He was a committed feminist, and in this, as in
so much else, his faith and conviction gave me strength in
the dark hours of my life. That he died during Passover,
which Jewish tradition suggests is proof of one's status as a
tzaddik, a righteous, saintly person, seems appropriate.

Not long before he died, he and I recalled a conversation
that took place shortly after the birth of my daughter, his
only granddaughter, named for his mother, Kathie. He had
then expressed his concern about her future in a nation,
indeed in a world, where her blackness might prove as dangerous as our Jewishness had already proven to us. It is not
overstating the case to say that America was, in 1951, still a
profoundly racist country, and he could scarcely bear the
idea that this child, so precious to us not only for herself but
for the fact that she represented all that Hitler had spared of

a next generation in our entire family, would have to battle both anti-Semitism and antiblack racism — two monstrous heads of a multiheaded evil.

We talked about how proud he had been, almost eighteen years later, when her secondary-school yearbook, with a page devoted to each graduating student, displayed how well she had integrated loyalty to both her heritages, the symbols of her activism: a star of David, the black-power fist, and the indication of her leadership in the socialist-Zionist youth group, Hashomer Hazair. Even though the miles between us and the financial barrier to frequent visits were hard for him to bear, he took pride in her becoming an African studies major at Hebrew University of Jerusalem. His hope — our hope — was that she might one day be a factor in renewing the ties of friendship between the two peoples whose future is hers.

And it wasn't that he, my father and my teacher, was any more blind than his daughter or her daughter to the faults of the earthly Israel, which like all nation-states is imperfect. He fully supported my efforts, as a progressive Zionist activist, in speeches, articles, and many conferences and meetings, to work in cooperation with the Israeli peace movement, and all those forces in the Jewish state and the Diaspora fighting for what David Ben-Gurion once described as the "three things worth living and also dying for: a Jewish state, a Jewish-Arab covenant, a socialist regime."

But as my father's life drew to its end, the desperation returned for him in the many signs that anti-Semitism was again oozing out of every gutter of the world, even in places where there were no longer Jews, even in places where there had never been any Jews. And so this man, who prayed and encouraged us to work for the day when the people of Africa and Asia and the Arab world would throw off Western colonialism, lived to see a world where some of the children of our ancient and modern oppressors and murderers, and the children of some they had oppressed, were suddenly in league against us, as at Entebbe; and as the left, of which we felt ourselves to be a moderate part, became no more reliable than the right, even using against us the rhetoric of our greatest suffering in a kind of Orwellian double-speak (Israelis fighting for their lives are called Nazis and Arabs fighting other Arabs are respected world leaders). Thus he whispered to me, "they will never let us live, it will never go away, they hate us too much." And he meant the world, for he feared for Kathie, and for her two boys, and for the future and survival of the Jewish people and of Israel, inseparable from each other.

But in this I will force myself to be different from my blessed father. I didn't have the heart to remind him, as he lay dying, that despair is forbidden to us; but I will not allow myself to despair. Instead, as long as God gives me breath, I will fight: fight in the Jewish arena, for the Jewish people and Israel to be the nation of priests and the light unto the gentiles that our prophets foretold. I will fight simultaneously in other arenas, however hostile, however ignorant, or, as I hope is the case in this place, where sisterhood and shared concerns make understanding possible, to win allies for my cause, which is peace, justice, and equality, and which can never come about if the price is a new blood-sacrifice of the Jewish people or the Jewish state. Who but the mendacious and dangerously foolish believe that if only Israel would disappear, Arabs would stop killing Arabs; Druse, Muslim, and Christian Lebanese would stop killing each other; and all of the above would stop killing Palestinians who would also stop killing them and each other. Repressive governments all over the world would fall, if only the world was once again "Israel-rein," free of the "scourge of Zionism," free even of Jews, in that part of the vicious propaganda now being spewed out in a variety of forums, which I will document here as fully as time allows. And so, let me turn from the subjective to the objective. For the facts are so clear, so frighteningly clear, that one need do no more than state them.

In the last decade, a slimy network of old Nazi sympathizers and activists in Europe, along with neo-Nazi sympathizers in the United States and Latin America (sometimes allied with "white citizens councils" and their ilk), have written, published, and promoted a number of books claiming that the Holocaust is a hoax, a vast Jewish and/or Zionist plot — and we will see how these terms are used interchangeably at the convenience of our enemies — to create an atmosphere that will help Jews rip off the world, politically and financially. One of these books, widely promoted by this network, is by a professor of engineering at a major midwestern university; the author is fully tenured, safe, and secure.

Those whose major commitment is to academic freedom and the rights guaranteed by the First Amendment may be horrified by such books, but they believe that the issue of freedom of expression is paramount. It is indeed an important, delicate, and complex issue. So is anti-Semitism.

In Western Europe, much of the soil is soaked with Jewish blood. There were "righteous gentiles," those Christians who risked their lives to save Jews and who are honored at the avenue bearing their name in Jerusalem at the Yad Vashem Holocaust museum and research center. But in Europe there were also many in the Christian leadership, institutions, and population who cheered the Nazis on, even when not actively assisting them in what Lucy Davidowicz has so eloquently called "The War Against the Jews." And there continue to be those who want to finish the Nazi task.

In my native Austria, Hitler found his most adoring audience; and Cardinal Innitzer, the highest prelate of the Catholic church, personally welcomed Hitler to Vienna. In August 1981, two persons were killed and twenty wounded when worshipers leaving a Bar Mitzvah at one of the few remaining synagogues in downtown Vienna were attacked by Arab terrorists hurling hand grenades and firing machine guns into the congregation, containing mostly old survivors and a few young children. The attackers insisted this was a legitimate "Zionist" target.

But when a homemade bomb exploded outside a Jewish-owned shop in Salzburg a year later, just plain old-fashioned anti-Semitic pamphlets were found nearby. Similar attacks followed, again in Vienna, on the home of Nazi-hunter Simon Wiesenthal, as well as the home of Alexander Giese, a member of the Austria-Israel Society.

In July 1980 in Antwerp, Belgium, an Arab who said he was fighting "the Zionist enemy" hurled two hand grenades into a group of Jewish teenagers, clearly marked by their dress as Orthodox, who were waiting to board a bus for summer camp. One was killed and twenty were wounded. In October 1981 a van loaded with explosives blew up across the street from Antwerp's main synagogue, killing two women and wounding ninety-nine other people just before services were to begin. The group claiming responsibility was "Direct Action, Belgium Section," an anarchist group. No reason was given.

And in France, with its mixed history of love of liberty and hatred for the Jews, and with one of the largest Jewish populations left in Western Europe, the incidents of Jew hatred are endless — from the kinds of books and tracts described above to bombs hurled into Jewish synagogues, restaurants, and stores. There is a free-for-all among those claiming credit for spilling Jewish blood, from a right-wing group using the old-fashioned slogan "Death to the Jews" to others using the now more fashionable "Death to the Zionists." The groups and individuals involved in these murders and mutilations have described themselves as everything from Maoist to anarchist to fascist; it seems that the greatest political and ideological differences can be overcome when uniting against the common devil, whether you identify it as Jew or Zionist.

In the few cases I have cited, drawn from a long list, one

thing stands out. Overwhelmingly, the victims, whether killed outright, seriously wounded, or simply psychologically scarred, were neither secret agents for the Israeli government nor powerful international figures. They were "ordinary people," ordinary men, women, or children — and indeed some of the children were too young to have any sense of identity — whose crime was being Jewish, and therefore one may assume sympathetic to and supportive of Israel's right to exist: that is, Zionist.

Let me say a brief word here about the Soviet Union. It is no secret to those who know me well that I think red-baiting is destructive and dangerous. I believe in détente, and I am grateful to the Soviet Union for its heroic role in the struggle against the Nazi monster. Furthermore, some Jews found the policy of American government and business leaders toward Germany after World War II a little difficult to bear. We felt it incongruous that while the brave people of England were still coping with food rationing, America should be helping the sector of Germany it controlled to the quickest economic recovery in postwar Europe. In the early days after the war, the Russians sometimes protected us from murderous Polish peasants trying to lynch Jewish death-camp survivors. We knew how deep the roots of anti-Semitism ran in czarist Russia and were grateful when the Soviet Union eloquently voted yes at the United Nations to the question of establishing Israel.

Recently, however, the Soviet Union has become one of the world's greatest producers and distributors of anti-Semitic literature. Its basic themes are borrowed from *The Protocols of the Elders of Zion*, a forgery dating from czarist times that purports to be the minutes of meetings by a cabal of Jews masterminding the attempt to undermine existing governments and assume world domination. Adolf Hitler's *Mein Kampf* seems to have served as another source. Both books paint the Jew as alien, disloyal, subversive, inherently evil, and given to lust for money. Jewish control of banks and the media in a variety of countries is an oft-articulated theme. The styles vary from the crudest Sturmer-like cartoons and vulgar attacks on the Bible, the Talmud, rabbis, synagogues, and so forth, to vitriolic tirades against Israel which, under the guise of anti-Zionism, express well-known anti-Semitic calumnies. In 1983, with great publicity, an Anti-Zionist Committee of the Soviet People was formed, charging that the Jews who are Zionist are really subversive agents working with the CIA. The Soviet Government has in effect painted the Jews in the USSR as a suspect population and thus radically increased their vulnerability.

There are some 110 national and ethnic groups in the USSR. In their propaganda they have always prided themselves on being a small family of nations. And yet Jews are looked at not just as another different group but in fact as a group of pariahs. Anti-Semitic literature is translated into the languages of groups living in areas where no Jews live. And what is ultimately created is an assumption among Soviet people that the Jew is different and apart and in fact "tainted" and ought to be kept apart, as, for example, Jewish and non-Jewish students were recently separated for a mathematics examination!

Before moving to other major sources of anti-Jewish propaganda today, which will get us back to the question of what happened at Copenhagen and what must not happen in the future, I turn to one more example of the recent coincidence of the issue of academic freedom and the use of anti-Zionism as a screen for teaching materials dangerous to the Jewish people, along with the need for all communities to be sensitive to the poison spewed in their name. At the Stony Brook, Long Island, campus of the State University of New York, black South African professor Dr. Ernest Dube has taught a course called "The Politics of Race." In this course Professor Dube teaches that Zionism is racism and is comparable to other forms of racism like Nazism and apartheid. In interviews given since the issue was made public, Dube defended himself by saying:

> My students can tell you that I never said that all Zionists are racists. . . . Even if I had said that all Zionists are racists . . . . that would not mean that I am anti-Semitic. There are quite a number of Jews who are not Zionists.

I wonder whether Dube or his defenders in the African Studies Program at Stony Brook would agree to let a non-black person, or blacks rejected by the overwhelming number of black people, decide for black people who truly represents them, their best interest, or their liberation movement. Another question that must be raised is one about Dr. Dube's more famous — or infamous — department chair. For whatever the outcome of this controversy, it can be said of the professor that he has impressed even some of his critics with an effort to separate his feelings about Jews and his stance on Zionism, at least to his own satisfaction. Dube has been quoted as saying:

> When I was growing up in South Africa I developed an affinity for the Jews, who I found were the only white people willing to treat me like a human being. I had many close Jewish comrades during the days I was underground with the African National Congress.

But the chairperson of the African Studies Program is Amiri Baraka, the former LeRoi Jones, a man whose record as a professional anti-Semite, whose long ugly history and poetry is filled with the kind of obscene racism that would have earned him a place of honor at the side of Hitler, Himmler, and Goering. I find myself physically and emotionally unable to quote it for you here, but you may wish to read it for yourself if you doubt its evil impact.

Baraka admits he was once a simple anti-Semite but is now only a proud anti-Zionist. One wonders *how* he received this academic appointment, in view of his history as a promoter of racial hatred and violence. One also wonders what the non-Jewish response would be were Baraka's counterpart in the Jewish community, Rabbi Meir Kahane, the former head of the Jewish Defense League, to receive a comparable appointment to head a Jewish Studies Department at a comparable American or Israeli University.

An attorney who supports Baraka and Dube has been quoted as saying, "The fact that the great majority of the nations of the world voted in favor of the proposition that Zionism is racism in 1975 legitimizes teaching it as truth in an American university." I would like to remind those who would agree with that assessment that there was a time when power was in the hands of those who enslaved and colonized the third world and its people. At that time the nations of the world would have voted that people of color are inferior to Western Europeans. I would suggest to feminists who refused to let Jewish or Israeli women get a hearing at Copenhagen, that a similar vote in many parts of the world (particularly those parts of the world they claim so much to identify with) would result in a vote recommending that women's role is to obey, fathers first and then husbands. Would such majorities have made the decisions right or true?

Which brings me then to that place where the infamous vote was taken, the United Nations: the place where the representatives of nations that butcher each other's young men in the real world, unite to denounce "the Zionist entity." The war between Iraq and Iran continues, and the United Nations refuses seriously to discuss it, much less condemn it, as it so often and with such monotonous regularity condemns Israel. But the U.N. ambassadors unite to denounce Israel. The ambassador of Syria condemns Israel, although in the town of Hama, Syrians butchered more Muslim Arabs and destroyed more mosques than Israel has ever done in all its wars combined. But the ambassador of Syria joins with his brothers from Iraq, Iran, and others in their club to condemn the Jewish state.

Let me, for example, quote what was said by the envoy of Colonel Quaddafi, when on 8 December 1983, the Libyan representative spoke as follows:

> We are convinced that the Zionist entity will be ousted from this hall, as was Formosa. It is high time for the United Nations and the United States in particular to realize that the Jewish Zionists here in the United States attempt to destroy Americans.

He continued:

> Look around New York. Who are the owners of pornographic film operations and houses? Is it not the Jews who are exploiting the American people and trying to debase them? If we succeed in eliminating that entity, we shall by the same token save the American and European peoples.

Zionism is the national liberation movement of the Jewish people. It has its roots in Scripture, as we wept for Jerusalem in our Babylonian captivity and swore to return — a pledge we made yearly for two thousand years, a faith that kept us whole through persecution and pogrom, through our Golden Age in Spain and through the longer periods when there seemed to be no light at all. Though political Zionism was most often expressed in secular terms (particularly by mainstream Zionism), to despise Zionism is to despise Judaism and the Jewish people.

Jews who turn back every criticism of a particular Israeli government or policy as a manifestation of anti-Semitism are wrong and self-defeating, and should read again the story of King Lear and his daughters. Right wing theological and political support of Israel often has dubious underpinnings and unhealthy motivation; thoughtful criticism from long-standing liberal friends may often be more loving in intent. But let there be no mistake that the language of hate and destruction, language that questions the right of Israel to exist, no matter what its source, is the language of the anti-Semite. Four hundred thousand Jews, Zionists all — my daughter and her family among them — stood in the streets of Tel Aviv to protest the destruction of Palestinian lives at Sabra and Shatilla by Christian Phalangists. Who in the Arab world cared enough or was free enough to stand with us?

But do not misread our opposition to a particular government or its policies. Instead, help us to create a climate where the question will not so often be "why is Israel not doing more?" but "why are its enemies not doing their share to bring peace and justice closer?"

We have been discussing power and powerlessness in the world. My good friend Rabbi Arnold Jacob Wolf speaks for me and my loved ones and friends in the Israeli peace movement when, writing in *Christianity and Crisis*, he says, "Powerlessness means becoming victims, power means learning how to treat decently those who are weaker than oneself." He goes on to suggest that Israel has not yet done well enough, but asks, "has the Soviet Union, or the United States or France?" Yet no one follows up criticism of those nations with the suggestion that they should cease to exist!

Finally, anti-Semitism, swathed in the poisonous garb of anti-Zionism, has become the new lingua franca of international politics, exploited by extremists of the left and right, by those who pose as revolutionaries and religious leaders, by third-world totalitarians as well as self-styled Western "progressives." Too often, in recent years, language dangerous to the Jewish people has been commonplace in the halls of the United Nations and at meetings organized under its auspices. If Copenhagen was deeply disturbing to most Jewish women, indeed to many women of faith, it was because the struggle of women's rights has not yet produced a universal rejection of the cancer almost as old as anti-feminism, anti-Semitism.

In closing, I say again that Jews who call every critic of Israeli government policies anti-Semitic are wrong—strategically, tactically, and most important, morally. But there is a greater wrong—the wrong that the world permits, that the United Nations permits, that many of the women at Copenhagen permitted, of allowing the Jewish people of the latter half of the twentieth century, and the Jewish state born out of the ashes of the Holocaust, to be defamed, stereotyped, and held to standards never applied to other people and other nations.

Women of faith may not be able to influence everything that is happening in today's world, but we can try. And within at least the women's movement, we can and must make a difference.

15

A Black Woman's Perspective on Racism, Classism, Sexism, and Ageism

Elizabeth M. Scott

The U.S. Catholic Bishops' pastoral letter on war and peace begins by quoting "The Pastoral Constitution on the Church in the Modern World," a document of the Second Vatican Council which says that "the whole human race faces a *moment of supreme crisis* in its advance toward maturity."

I want to discuss racism, classism, sexism, and ageism as diseases in our domestic and international societies, broken cisterns which produce powerlessness. Individuals affected by these particular diseases might have said that as the human race works out its maturity, the systemic behavior and practices which perpetrate and perpetuate racism, sexism, classism, and ageism have indeed caused supreme crises in their lives. We must acknowledge the cost — to groups and to

The Reverend Elizabeth M. Scott formerly directed the Justice for Women Office in the Division of Church and Society of the National Council of Churches of Christ in the U.S.A. She currently is the pastor of St. James African Methodist Episcopal Church in New Kensington, Pennsylvania.

individuals — of these crimes and evils. The cost has been tremendous!

The violence permitted by human beings upon fellow human beings has been tremendous — astronomical — unbelievable and painful to know and witness: lynching, castration, hunger, starving, cold, poor education. People not able to compete; alone, without friend, family, or neighbor; imprisoned because of the institutionalized devastation of their lives. Tearing and ripping of family life because of the need to sustain a privileged class. Poverty of the greatest, cruelest kind — poverty in the midst of plenty. Dire poverty: no housing, no food, no clothing, no jobs, just abuse of humankind.

Did I say no jobs? Third-world women — the new "factory girls" — are providing vast pools of cheap labor for undisciplined, unrestricted, globe-trotting corporations. They are subjected to the violence of poor health and safety conditions, inadequate work surroundings, destruction and lack of appreciation for their third-world cultures — all for the sake of the profit of the few. (Or is it greed?) No jobs? There are jobs for "hospitality girls" — tourism profits made at the expense of young women in prostitution. There is economic suppression, and sexism toward women on the global assembly line. Women are utilized as farmers and water carriers. The feminization of poverty is an everyday reality.

Poverty is disproportionately borne by people of color, as racial discrimination continues to exist along with high unemployment. There will be many poor men of color in the year 2000 — but for the greater part, women will bear the burden of poverty.

As divorce rates rise and childbirth occurs out of marital relationships, women are more likely to carry primary responsibility for supporting themselves and their children. Meanwhile, the elderly, while they represent a significant population in this country, are still an extremely vulnerable group. Imprisonment of the elderly is on the rise — because of property crimes that are directly related to economic disadvantages. All of this suffering is expressed in words like racism, classism, sexism, and ageism.

Powerlessness is the end result for groups of people caught in the jaws of these social diseases. But then powerlessness is a growing phenomenon. Almost all people are experiencing some form of powerlessness in their lives: black women, teenagers, the elderly. This causes us to look *beyond* the issues of racism, sexism, classism, and ageism.

There is not much need to spell out further the conditions of human suffering caused by these evils; rather we should examine the moment of supreme crisis as the whole human race advances toward maturity, to determine the moment's positives as well as its negatives. The threat of nuclear destruction does not change the existence of racism, sexism, classism, and ageism, but it does serve as a different lens through which to view these evils. The supreme crisis of the threat of world destruction intensifies the need to rid the world of its diseases, crimes, and evils. The social decision before us and the generations to come is this: How will ethical and technical arenas interact? We must learn to see the two as inseparable.

We are not powerless in efforts to weave these arenas together, but in weaving them we must be creative, adventuresome, bold, and fair. We must recognize new possibilities. May I share several of Betty Friedan's suggestions from her book *The Second Stage*? Friedan makes three important points about the second stage of the women's movement. First, it cannot be seen in terms of women alone, or of our separate personhood. Second, it involves coming to new terms with the family, and with love and work. Third, it requires us to transcend the battle for equal power in institutions; instead, we must restructure institutions and transform the nature of power itself.

Admittedly, we are in a stage of world transformation.

The basis of concern in reshaping the world order cannot carry evils past and present into the future if we are to mature in a healthy fashion.

As the women's movement searches its soul for a right future, for something other than women alone and our separate personhood, so must we all begin to embrace the spiritual concepts of inclusiveness, crossing racial boundaries, overcoming sex and class limitations, yes, and overcoming even the myths of eternal youth.

We can help redefine the terms of family, love, and work. The values underlying these terms can be reworked and we can do it — we are not powerless. We must transform the nature of power and restructure institutions for the sake of love of self, for the sake of love of neighbor, for the sake of love of God. We can transform individualism into real relationships with each other and with God. We can heal relationships and build community. We can transform society by healing relationships of injustice and oppression.

As a new world order shapes itself, we must not leave its formation to the intellectuals and the political elite. Those of us caught in the jaws of the -isms which we discuss, must become actively involved in the movement for a new world order.

There are two reasons why we must be involved. They are stated as clearly as they can be stated by Gerald and Patricia Mische, authors of *Toward a Human World Order*. The first reason for involvement is that the input of local grassroots experiences and of citizens' natural savvy concerning human relations and practical wisdom, provides a vital dimension of reality that is essential if any world-order system is to work. These elements complement the knowledge and experience of the "experts." The second reason is strategic. A more human world-order system will not materialize without the understanding and assent of the citizens. It will not happen if it is not the will of the people.

The human race now shares in a worldwide civilization. As transnational corporations bring us global factories, we as women of faith must insist on a more humane, more loving, more caring global community. Human survival is in a supreme crisis today, but so is the maintenance of a kind of life that is worth surviving for.

Ours is the task of defining and instituting distributive justice. Food and energy are absolutely essential to life. Not only must we answer the question of *how* to distribute the world's resources; we must be sure of why it is necessary to redistribute.

The potential threat of world destruction does not end with the reduction of military arms, but with providing all the people of the world with a stake in peace. North-South relations must be regarded as having the same importance as East-West relations in world affairs.

Racism, classism, sexism, and ageism are problems most often viewed as domestic problems. But daily we are becoming aware of the interrelatedness of domestic and global issues. We must now weave a global fabric for a world community based on social justice and human priorities. We must cease reinforcing the paternalism and empirical domination of the West.

Our task must be to use our vision of the concrete realities to transform others — not to conquer them, but to persuade. Science has made the world a neighborhood, but it will take love to make it a sisterhood, a brotherhood, a community of peace with justice.

The question posed by our supreme crisis is this: Can we love well enough?

16

The Feminization of Poverty

Mimi Alperin

When I was growing up in the 1950s, every mother's dream for her grown daughter was that she would meet and marry a nice successful young man who would support her while she raised their children. College and academic achievement were encouraged as ends in themselves. Parents took great pride in our scholastic success, but never dreamed that we would ever have to use our educations to support ourselves — God forbid! How could they have known then how many of us daughters of the fifties would become the sole breadwinners of our families, raising our children often with little or no support from their fathers and with little preparation for the world of paid work?

Belief in the Cinderella myth was not exclusive to middle-class families like mine. Daughters of the poor were not better prepared for the real world than we were. Even black women who had been forced by economic circumstances to enter the paid work force in numbers double that of white women, dreamed that their daughters would be able to as-

Mimi Alperin, member of a Conservative Jewish congregation, chairs the executive committee of the board of governors at the American Jewish Committee. Formerly she chaired the Interreligious Affairs Commission of the American Jewish Committee.

sume the traditional woman's role of mother and homemaker. Marriage, we were taught, was the assurance of economic security. A woman who worked outside the home—and 30 percent of all married women did, in 1960—did so to supplement her family income. Most of this 30 percent were women over the age of thirty-five whose children were in school. Inflation, rising expectations, and a desire for self-fulfillment were the primary motivating forces propelling women into the work force in the 1950s. Women didn't have to think about how little they were paid, or how few the opportunities for advancement, as long as their salaries helped to buy a second car or a family vacation.

My fifteen-year-old daughter's world of the 1980s bears little resemblance to the "Ozzie and Harriet" or "Leave It to Beaver" world of my adolescence. The typical family of the fifties—working father, homemaking mother, 2.3 children, and one dog—represents approximately 15 percent of all families today. The promise that marriage would mean economic security has given way to the cruel reality that for most women and their dependent children today marriage is the *only* way to stay out of poverty. My mother never could have anticipated that motherhood would become a dangerous occupation, offering no job security, no benefits (except psychic), and a financially insecure old age.

Divorce or separation from a male breadwinner (or his death) has virtually guaranteed economic hardship, if not poverty, for millions of women and their children, creating a new reality in this country called "the feminization of poverty." Diana Pearce, the sociologist who identified and named this trend, wrote in 1978 that from 1969 to 1978 an additional one hundred thousand women with children fell below the poverty line in *each* of those years. According to the President's Advisory Council on Economic Opportunity, if this increase were to continue, by the year 2000 the entire poverty population in the United States would consist of women and their children.

Old age is a dreadful prospect for many women. A "retired mother" will probably survive her husband, having nursed him through illness, and will find herself on her own with a median income of $4,226. If she is "lucky" enough to survive beyond the age of seventy-five, she has a median income of $3,000 to look forward to.

A Rand Corporation study estimates that 21 percent of all families today are headed by one female parent — and she is often an unwed teenager. In 1979 more than one in four babies born in the black community were born to teenagers — one in seven for whites. No longer a social stigma, bearing a child is often more acceptable than having an abortion. Marriage to the father — once the almost inevitable consequence of pregnancy — is no longer desirable when the father is likely to be an unemployed teenager. Whatever the reason for the increase in teenage pregnancy, the young woman's options are forever limited, often to a life of poverty — not to mention the tragically limited future of the child born to a child.

It is clear in studying the phenomenon of the feminization of poverty that the poverty and economic vulnerability of women is most often directly related to the characteristic of being female in our society. Men are poor for reasons unrelated to being male, such as lack of education or technical training, involvement in drugs or crime, or racism. Women, however, are poor because they bear children and raise them, because there is little day care, and little or no child support; poor because they are adolescent parents or because they face sexism in the workplace. For men the answer to poverty is jobs, but the solution to female poverty is far more complicated. A woman on welfare can't hold a job if there is no one to care for her children. Work incentives in the welfare system therefore have no effect on the majority of recipients who are women.

Even if a woman has a job it is no guarantee that she will be able to pull herself above the poverty level. Fifty-three percent of women who work full-time, year round, earn under $5,000 per year. A recent profile in *The New York Times* of a single working parent describes the struggle of one woman to support her family. In 1978 Mrs. B., the mother of five children, was divorced. She earned $2.65 per hour at a bakery where she worked fifteen hours a week. An additional $150 a week in child support put her income $3,140 above the median income for families headed by women and $1,600 above the poverty level for a family of six. She also qualified for federal day care, food stamps, and infant nutrition programs. But by 1982 her income had risen slowly to $6.20 an hour and eligibility requirements were revised, causing Mrs. B. to lose all federal assistance. Last spring she took a second part-time job paying $2.65 an hour to make up for some of the lost assistance. She said:

> In a way it seems that I am being punished for the improvements I have made in my situation. The more I made, the more aid was taken away, never mind that costs were rising too.

Mrs. B. is one of the lucky single parents because her former husband helps to support their children; she would not need federal assistance at all if she received a decent wage for the work she performs.

A study by the National Advisory Council on Economic Opportunity titled "Causes and Cures for Poverty: Men versus Women" characterizes our economic system as having dual labor markets and dual welfare systems. The primary labor market, composed disproportionately of white males, offers high wages, fringe benefits, job security, and unions. When a worker loses his job, the primary welfare sector views benefits as a right, offers guaranteed federal benefits, assures privacy, indexes benefits to the cost of living, and doesn't require the depletion of all resources to qualify. The secondary labor market, disproportionately minorities and women, is characterized by low wages, little job security, part-time and seasonal work, few fringe benefits, a low rate of unionization, and little protection from arbitrary employers. Loss of a job in this sector means minimal support; benefits are viewed as a privilege rather than a right; levels of benefits vary from state to state; privacy is often violated, because there is no indexing of benefits and one must prove oneself a pauper in order to qualify. An unemployed truck driver receives unemployment benefits; an unemployed waitress goes on welfare.

This gloomy picture I've painted doesn't square with the media portrayal of women in the 1980s — sleek, suited in three-piece gabardine, striding purposefully into an executive boardroom carrying a leather briefcase. This image represents a very small minority of women who have broken the barrier to the male work world. In 1971 4 percent of all lawyers and judges were female — today, 1 percent. As the author of the recently published pamphlet "Poverty in the American Dream" puts it, "Few women enter corporate boardrooms in any capacity besides secretary or cleaning woman." Women today earn less than they did in 1955 — fifty-nine cents for every dollar earned by a man, as compared to sixty-five cents thirty years ago. Eighty percent of the female work force is clustered in the lowest paying, "pink-collar" occupations — clerical, retail sales, domestic work, restaurant and food service, nursing and elementary school teaching. College-educated females earn less than a man with an eighth-grade education. Whatever work women do, it is consistently undervalued and underpaid when compared with the work that men perform. In 1980 female salespersons averaged $176 a week, while male salespersons averaged $337 a week. The more a job category is dominated by women, the less the job pays, with compensation decreasing by $42 for every additional percentage point of women employed.

Because of job segregation, the equal-pay act has had very little effect on equalizing the salaries of women with men. The pervasive attitude underlying pay inequity is that women and the work they perform, whether it be in the home as a wife and mother or in the marketplace as a paid worker, is somehow worth less than the accomplishments of men. This undervaluation, which is deeply rooted in our culture and our traditions, both legal and religious, is significantly responsible for the economic vulnerability of women today. Margaret Mead pointed out just how pervasive this attitude is when she wrote that in some societies men fish and women weave; in others women fish and men weave. But in both types of society the work men do is valued more highly than that which is done by women.

Some attitudes have changed since I grew up in the fifties. My daughter knows that Prince Charming, if he ever comes along, can easily turn back into a frog. She will never be as vulnerable as my generation was. In some ways I feel very sad for her generation. I wonder how many will have the luxury of being full-time mothers if that is what they want to do. Not many. It's a dangerous option. And we have just begun to calculate the damage to children of divorce, of poverty, of female heads of families: high rates of truancy, and the phenomenon of latch-key children.

Before my daughter is ready to go out on her own, we have a lot of work to do to overcome the institutionalized sexism that affects every woman, cutting across boundaries of age, race, religion, and economic class. If there is anything that should bind us together as sisters, it is this shared vulnerability. We as women of faith can bring to the struggle for economic equality the unique perspective of loving respect for our religious faith, along with an ethical and critical approach where our traditions fail us as women. Thus, we can point to the role religion has played in demeaning and undervaluing women. It is my hope that we will consider taking a close look at what is happening to the American family, an institution in desperate need of help. We could be an effective, progressive moral voice countering those who call themselves "profamily" but who ignore the hard reality of today's family units.

PART FOUR

An Interreligious
Worship Service

In this section, Norma U. Levitt describes the crafting and experiencing of an interreligious worship service. The text of that service follows.

17

Preparing an Interreligious Worship Service

Norma U. Levitt

Three women met for the first planning session: a Protestant, a Jew, and a Roman Catholic. They mentioned that a supportive spirit must have guided them for their appointment to fit so neatly into busy work and travel schedules. Having made their date by telephone one afternoon, they met the following morning, just two days after one of them had returned from the Soviet Union and on the day when another was to leave the city that very afternoon.

The group convened in New York City in a lounge at Marymount College where most of their subsequent meetings would also be held. At the end of two hours of discussion and brainstorming, there emerged a basic pattern for an interreligious service. Plans included the lighting of candles, music, an opening prayer on oppression and freedom, and thankfulness to God for the blessing of a group of women coming together to speak freely and to explore concepts of

NORMA U. LEVITT is United Nations nongovernmental-organization representative of the World Union for Progressive Judaism. She is also honorary president of the National Federation of Temple Sisterhoods and president of the World Conference on Religion and Peace.

power and powerlessness. Following a reference to a biblical theme, the service would then include a responsive reading related to issues of concern to women of faith, and a prayer of petition for spiritual guidance in facing life's complexities. After a period of silent meditation, a music solo, and a psalm read in unison, there would be a roll call of the women in attendance. But this would not be a call of their own names. Rather, it would be a calling out of the names of well-known or little-known women who had empowered them and others to serve life's goals. This roll call would later be underscored — by having participants write names on a long scroll of paper and by other features of the subsequent celebration.

Many themes and methods that would be developed later were touched on during the first planning meeting. The three women spoke of personal power, and power together. They asked, how much can we do for ourselves and how much does our power come from God? They reflected that sometimes when we are most powerless, we most open ourselves to power, perhaps through opening our life to the power of spirit. Believing that women sitting next to each other, even if strangers to each other, might be sources of mutual empowerment, the committee sought ways to encourage openness to others about deeply held concerns, in order to establish connections.

Women of faith are required to be active, to focus on issues, the planners agreed. So there was need in the service for a call to action, a preparation to hear and to do — to be involved on behalf of the destitute and abandoned, not only by helping to give assistance and hope, but also through strengthening their will to act for themselves.

The planners spoke of light, the Hebrew concept of Shekhinah, the spirit that links God with the world, as well as developing an atmosphere of freedom to differ, simultaneously with strengthening the bonds of connectedness. They said that, although the nations seem to be on a collision course, there is a longing for peace, *shalom*, for a sense of wholeness in the world. People are tired, one woman said; they need a sense of energy, of excitement, of new possibilities. The committee determined the need for music, movement, and dance.

By the time of the second committee meeting, one month later, two additional women had agreed to join the planning process: a sister who had recently graduated from a theological seminary, as well as having been active in interreligious groups; and a Protestant dancer-choreographer and writer of several books on dance as well as director of an ecumenical group of dancers who explore spirituality in dance for all denominations. A psalm was chosen and writing assignments were accepted. A decision was made to create a truly interreligious service, not by letting each person write a section from her tradition which would remain untouched, but rather through group interaction and cooperation on every section, no matter who had written the first draft. The name "Gathering" was adopted.

At the third meeting, attended by all five women, some prayers were brought for group suggestions, at which time a new element was added. One of the women, sensitive to antifeminist language in liturgy, pointed out that we often assign "commanding" language to God. "Let us listen and ask God to empower us," she said, "to enable us, to comfort, and to nurture." For prayers already written in language long held sacred, moving from "command" to cooperation might have been a divisive experience. Instead, the other committee members learned and laughed with their colleague who had raised their consciousness concerning new language in prayer. Aware of the long-accepted masculine pronouns, one of the sisters remarked, "I ran out of names for God, so I asked assistance from a reliable resource person, the rabbi whom I have invited to teach some sessions of my class."

By the final planning meeting, the dancer brought several additional suggestions. First, she showed simple movements in which all conference attendees might participate during the opening service, with gestures of receiving the light of candles. For the dance presentation, she suggested as a theme the life of Anne Frank, the young Dutch Jewish girl who with her family was hidden by Christian friends from the Nazis in a dark attic during World War II.

By the time the order of the service "Gathering" was ready, a problem surfaced: all the music sounded Christian; there was no Jewish music, nor any sheet music available. This oversight was rectified when the pianist and choir quickly learned a Jewish tune. When the "Roll Call of Women" was reached during the service, there were pauses to encourage the further remembering of names of women who had been a source of inspiration. From around the room came these names, first haltingly and quietly, then with the assurance of acceptance. The openness of the creative process continued until the last moment of the service.

During the evening celebration, our dance leader performed "Choose Life" on a bare stage. Her dance expressed the life, fears, hopes, and death in a concentration camp of young Anne Frank. The dance and the memories it stirred evoked tears from many participants.

The naming of women continued after the dance. Touched by the story of Anne Frank, participants gathered in two circles. The inner circle faced the outer one, each person speaking the name of a woman who had empowered her, then moved to another partner to speak another name. Many felt the presence of the named women filling the hall. Participants remembered depths of long-forgotten meaning and opened these experiences to their companions.

What was learned by the planning process of these services of meditation and celebration? The hours spent together by the small planning committee had built mutual acceptance of individual differences and each person's rich spiritual resources. Because of this slow building of trust and appreciation, the process of creation remained open until the last moment. The sharing of work over a long time, acceptance of the differences of another while feeling free to express one's own diversities — this shimmering but strong ribbon of experience brought understanding, creativity, and enjoyment.

18

Gathering:
An Interreligious Worship Service

Prepared by Virginia Baron;
Carla De Sola (dance);
Norma Levitt; Joan Ronayne, R.S.H.M.;
Catherine Vincie, R.S.H.M. (music)

Musical Prelude

Lighting of the Candles   (liturgical dance)

Opening Prayer:

Eternal Spirit, we believe in your limitless fidelity to us; deepen our faith within us. We believe in your absolute trust; enliven our hope. We believe in the certainty of your love; infuse new love into us.

We come before you as women of faith; look on our impoverished spirit and empower us to fullness of faith. Look on the gifts you have given us and inspire us in the creative use of them. Look on the oppressed and unfree areas of our lives; call us into new freedom. Look on those issues which unite us; let the unity of your life flow through us to one another.

God of all creation, we believe that you have an eternal care for all of your people; guide us as women of faith to promote your love wherever it is overshadowed or destroyed by divisiveness, destruction, war, or oppression of any kind. You are a God of peace; open our minds and hearts and help us to be peacemakers. You are the source of our inspiration, you are our strength, you are our light and our hope; may we always remember to call on you, especially in times of powerlessness, weakness, and uncertainty. We praise and thank you for your eternal goodness and for the abundance of life you continue to give us.

We love you especially for the gentle ways in which you constantly re-create us, and we beg you to bring about the true recognition of women everywhere as daughters of God, called to the fullness of life in you, and sharers in the building of your sovereignty on earth.

Accept our prayer, Adonai, which comes from hearts hungry for you and for your justice; hearts also humbled by our own many infidelities, yet confident in your goodness and compassion which are beyond all human understanding. Amen.

Responsive Reading:

Psalm 103 (adapted)
RIGHT SIDE: Bless God, my soul,
bless God's name, all that is in me!
Bless Adonai, my soul,
and remember all God's kindnesses

ALL: *and remember all God's kindnesses*

LEFT SIDE: in forgiving all your
                              offenses,
in curing all your diseases,
in redeeming your life from the
                              pit,
in crowning you with love and
                              tenderness,
in filling your years with
                              prosperity,
in renewing your youth with
                              strength.

ALL: *in renewing your youth with strength*

RIGHT SIDE: God, who does
what is right,
is always on the side of the
oppressed;
God's spirit revealed strength to
the people of
Israel.

ALL: *God's spirit revealed strength to the people of Israel*

LEFT SIDE: Adonai is tender and
                              compassionate,
slow to anger, most loving;
Adonai never treats us, never
                              punishes us,
as our guilt and sins deserve.

ALL: *as our guilt and sins deserve*

RIGHT SIDE: No less than the
height of
heaven over
earth
is the greatness of God's love for
those of dutiful fear.
Adonai takes our sins farther away
than the east is from the west.

ALL: *Adonai takes our sins farther away than the east is from the west*

LEFT SIDE: As tenderly as
                         parents treat their
                         children
so God treats those who are loving;
Adonai knows what we are made
                         of,
always remembers we are dust.
We last no longer than grass,
no longer than a wild flower do we
                         live,
one gust of wind and we are gone,
never to be seen there again.

ALL: *we are gone, never to be seen there again*

                    RIGHT SIDE: Yet Adonai's love
                                          for all people
             lasts from all eternity and forever,
                          it extends to our children's
                                          children
                     as long as they remember the
                                          covenant.
             Bless God, all angels, all people.
             Bless God, all creatures in every
                          part of the earth and sea.

ALL: *Bless God, my soul!*

PERIOD OF SILENCE

MUSIC OF THE SPIRIT

RESPONSIVE READING:

READER: Grant us power, O God, to right the wrongs which we inherit,

ALL: the sins we perpetuate, the oppression we endure.

READER: for the prejudice of race against race,

ALL: and for distorting facts to fit our theories;

READER: for the alienation of class against class,

ALL: and for maintaining silence and indifference;

READER: for the deception of sexes against each other,

ALL: and for denying responsibility for our own and others' misfortunes;

READER: for the disdain against those whose age disturbs us,

ALL: and for pretending to emotions we do not feel;

READER: for the aggression of religious prejudice and the denial of religious freedom,

ALL: and for deceiving ourselves and others with half truths;

READER: for keeping the poor in chains of poverty,

ALL: and turning a deaf ear to the cry of the oppressed;

READER: for waging war and supporting violence,

ALL: and for appeasing aggressors;

READER: for poisoning by cynicism,

ALL: and for withholding trust and love; forgive us, O God.

READER: You, O God, have fashioned us in your image, to be co-creators with you in a world where we can help to make a better life.

ALL: Teach us to right the wrongs we inherit, the sins we perpetuate,

READER: the oppression we endure.

ALL: Give us the assurance that each one of us matters and that every action counts.

READER: Grant us hope, to lift us out of a sense of powerlessness.

ALL: Hope sustains us when we rise each morning, when we undertake every task, when we turn to our neighbor in trust.

READER: As we consider our concerns, O God,

ALL: grant us hope,
               grant us power,
               grant us peace.

Hymn to be sung during the Roll Call of Women:

Gather Us In

Here in this place, new light is streaming,
Now is the darkness vanished away.
See, in this space, our fears and our dreamings
Brought here to you in the light of this day.
Gather us in, the lost and forsaken,
Gather us in, the blind and the lame,
Call to us now, and we shall awaken,
We shall arise at the sound of our name.

We are the young, our lives are a mystery,
We are the old, who yearn for your face.
We have been sung throughout all of history,
Called to be light to the whole human race.
Gather us in, the rich and the haughty,
Gather us in, the proud and the strong,
Give us a heart so meek and so lowly,
Give us the courage to enter the song.

Not in the dark of buildings confining,
Not in some heaven light years away.
But here in this space, the new light is shining
Now is the kingdom, now is the day.
Gather us in, and hold us forever,
Gather us in, and make us your own.
Gather us in, all peoples together,
Fire of life in our flesh and our bone.

Roll Call of Women:

As women of faith, we stop to remember women who have gone before:

women who have left their mark on our lives, on the lives of others in society, and on history . . .

women whose lives give us courage when our spirits are burnt out . . .

women who would not accept definitions assigned to them by tradition when it meant confining their aspirations . . .

women who were willing to clear new paths in unfamiliar territory for the sake of their families or their communities . . .

women who walked in the light of their own energy and enthusiasm to create institutions of hope for the lost, the sick, and the forgotten . . .

women who have dared to be all they could be, in the dark times and in the bright times.

All: "Gather Us In" (first verse)

We pause to remember women we never knew whose lives have inspired us:

Naming of Names

Silence

All: "Gather Us In" (second verse)

We pause to remember women we have known whose encouragement and example have pushed us to the limits of ourselves:

Naming of Names

Silence

All: "Gather Us In" (third verse)

We pause to remember women we know who may be unknown to the world but who have poured their power and love and blessings on us:

Naming of Names

Silence

As women of faith, we give thanks for the lives of all the women we have named. We ask the God of creation to dwell in us so that we may be a light for those who come after us.

All: "Gather Us In" (all verses)

BENEDICTION   (liturgical dance)

Appendix:
Guidelines for Forming
a Local Group of
Women of Faith

1. Start with a core group of Jewish, Catholic, Protestant, and Islamic women interested in interreligious dialogue. Try to build trust by sharing your stories, with emphasis on your faith-experience. Create a mailing list, starting with the core group and reaching out to interested women from a diversity of religious traditions.

2. Adopt a statement of purpose to guide your planning of meeting topics and actions. Here, for purposes of comparison, is the statement of purpose of the Women of Faith in the 80s Task Force, adopted in 1981:

   We are a representative group of women of faith from the Jewish, Christian, and Islamic traditions, who seek better understanding of each other's commitments, cooperative

---

These guidelines were prepared by Virginia Ramey Mollenkott, in cooperation with a Women of Faith group that met at Riverside Church on 26 September 1986; and with help from the Membership Guidelines of the Women's Interfaith Dialogue on the Middle East (Philadelphia, Pennsylvania); "Women of Faith in the 80s: Beginnings and Early History," by Norma U. Levitt; and "A Proposal for a Working Understanding of the Task Force of Women of Faith in the 80s," prepared in 1985 by Mimi Alperin, Sarah Cunningham, Inge Lederer Gibel, Joan Ronayne, and Jeanne Audrey Powers (committee chair).

action on matters of mutual concern, dialogue on issues related to religious perspectives, and sharing of resources through research and network relationships among women of faith throughout the country.

3. Emphasize that the purpose of the meetings is to dialogue, not to debate. Value diversity.

4. Because continuity is important, members should commit themselves to regular attendance, and the issue of occasional guests should be carefully considered.

5. As necessary, membership fees and organizational officers may be decided upon. The task force in New York has kept itself as informal as possible, and that is probably a wise procedure for other groups as well. Should the group decide to hire a professional facilitator, dues or outside funding might become necessary. Local religious institutions might be willing to help support the group.

6. Meetings may be structured around a specific topic, with a brief, carefully researched presentation followed by dialogue that airs the views of the various women, rooted as they are in their diverse religious traditions. Topics may include the problems women face within their religious institutions; or critical social problems such as racism, sexism, classism, ageism, and militarism; or Middle Eastern concerns. A particular book or article may be chosen as the focus of discussion, in which case members are responsible to do the reading in advance of the meeting. Chairing of the meetings should probably be rotated from member to member.

7. As the group feels prepared to do so, it may wish to plan and sponsor public meetings concerning areas of interreli-

gious interest, or to take a public stand concerning matters that call for interreligious comment. Individual members may find it possible to lend their names and energies to issues that may not affect them personally but that are of deep concern to one of their sisters. At times, such issues may require special actions so that a common mind can be expressed by the group (for instance, in a letter to newspapers, or to religious or public officials). However, it is not appropriate for any one woman to "use" the group for her own individual ends.

8. Register the contact person for your group with the Women of Faith Facilitator, American Jewish Committee, 165 East 56 Street, New York, New York 10022. Such registration will assure that your group will receive notice of any national conferences that may be planned, and notice of any future publications. It will make your group part of an interreligious women's network.

9. Bear in mind that with dedicated membership and careful nurturing, your local Women of Faith group can become not only an oasis of trust and strength in a desert of suspicion, but also a model for peacemaking, coalition building, and joint action. Such action can empower women both inside and outside religious traditions to provide leadership in a world yearning for justice, peace, and understanding. We are in the midst of a movement bigger than we know. Our power is in knowing our roots, what we are intended to be, and the difference we can make.